Reformation Observances: 1517–2017

Reformation Observances: 1517–2017

EDITED BY Philip D. W. Krey

FOREWORD BY John A. Radano

PREFACE BY Christopher W. Bellitto

CASCADE *Books* · Eugene, Oregon

REFORMATION OBSERVANCES: 1517–2017

Copyright © 2017 Wipf and Stock Publishers. All rights reserved. Except for brief quotations in critical publications or reviews, no part of this book may be reproduced in any manner without prior written permission from the publisher. Write: Permissions, Wipf and Stock Publishers, 199 W. 8th Ave., Suite 3, Eugene, OR 97401.

Cascade Books
An Imprint of Wipf and Stock Publishers
199 W. 8th Ave., Suite 3
Eugene, OR 97401

www.wipfandstock.com

PAPERBACK ISBN: 978-1-5326-1656-3
HARDCOVER ISBN: 978-1-4982-4041-3
EBOOK ISBN: 978-1-4982-4040-6

Cataloguing-in-Publication data:

Names: Krey, Philip D. W., editor | Belitto, Christopher M., preface | Radano, John A., foreword.

Title: Reformation observances : 1517–2017 / edited by Philip D. Krey ; preface by Christopher M. Belitto ; foreword by John A. Radano.

Description: Eugene, OR: Cascade Books, 2017 | Includes bibliographical references.

Identifiers: ISBN 978-1-5326-1656-3 (paperback) | ISBN 978-1-4982-4041-3 (hardcover) | ISBN 978-1-4982-4040-6 (ebook).

Subjects: LCSH: Reformation—History and criticism.

Classification: BR301 R42 2017 (print) | BR301 (ebook).

Manufactured in the U.S.A.   08/08/17

Unless otherwise noted, Scripture quotations come from the New Revised Standard Version Bible copyright © 1989 National Council of the Churches of Christ in the United States of America. Used by permission. All rights reserved worldwide.

Contents

List of Contributors / vii

Foreword: 2017—An Ecumenical Perspective / John A. Radano / ix

Preface: Remembering Luther—A Reformer in Church History / Christopher W. Bellitto / xxvii

Acknowledgments / xxxv

List of Abbreviations / xxxvii

Introduction / Philip D. W. Krey / xxxix

1. Martin Luther and the Lutheran Reformation—October 31, 1517–October 31, 2017: From Augustinian Monk and Doctor of the Church Attempting to Reform Catholic Theology in 1517 to *doctor communis* of the Church in 2017 / Philip D. W. Krey / 1

2. Martin Luther and the Episcopal Church / Robert W. Prichard / 24

3. Celebrating the Dynamic Legacy of the Reformation: An Indian Perspective / J. Jayakiran Sebastian / 43

4. The Five-Hundredth Anniversary of the Reformation: A Catholic Perspective / Jacob. W. Wood / 69

Contributors

Christopher M. Bellitto is Professor of History at Kean University in Union, New Jersey. He is co-editor of *Reassessing Reform: A Historical Investigation into Church Renewal* (2012) and author of *Renewing Christianity: A History of Church Reform from Day One to Vatican II* (2001).

Philip D. W. Krey is The Ministerium of New York Professor of Church History, emeritus at the Lutheran Theological Seminary at Philadelphia, Pennsylvania. He is Senior Pastor at St Andrews Lutheran Church in Perkasie, Pennsylvania. And he is the co-editor of *The Catholic Luther: His Early Writings* (2016).

Robert W. Prichard is The Arthur Lee Kinsolving Professor of Christianity in America and Instructor in Liturgics at the Virginia Theological Seminary, Alexandria, Virginia. He is the author of *A History of the Episcopal Church*, 3rd ed. (2014).

Monsignor **John A. Radano** is Adjunct Professor in the School of Theology, Seton Hall University, South Orange, New Jersey. From 1984 to 2008 he served as staff in the Pontifical Council for Promoting Christian Unity, Vatican City. He is the author of *Lutheran and Catholic Reconciliation on Justification* (2009).

CONTRIBUTORS

J. Jayakiran Sebastian is a Presbyter of the Church of South India and currently Dean of the Seminary and H. George Anderson Professor of Mission and Cultures at the Lutheran Theological Seminary at Philadelphia, Pennsylvania. He has been a Professor in the Department of Theology and Ethics at the United Theological College, Bangalore, India, where he was also the Chairperson of the Department and Dean of Doctoral Studies. He is the author of *Enlivening the Past: An Asian Theologian's Engagement with the Early Teachers of Faith* (2009).

Jacob W. Wood is Assistant Professor of Theology at the Franciscan University of Steubenville, Ohio. He is the author of *Speaking the Love of God: An Introduction to the Sacraments* (2016).

Foreword

2017: An Ecumenical Perspective

—John A. Radano

Many in the Christian world are now giving attention to commemorating or celebrating the 500th anniversary of the Reformation in 2017, and rightly so. It is a time for Christians to assess what they have learned from that period, and where they stand now. And this volume is a contribution to that.

The recent Lutheran and Catholic study, *From Conflict to Communion: Lutheran-Catholic Common Commemoration of the Reformation in 2017*[1] stated that a common ecumenical remembrance of the Lutheran Reformation is so important, but at the same time is so difficult. It is difficult because of the two ways in which the Reformation is seen today: "many Catholics associate the word 'Reformation' first of all with the division of the church, while many Lutheran Christians associate the word 'Reformation' chiefly with the rediscovery of the gospel, certainty of faith and freedom."[2] Obviously, Catholics cannot celebrate the division of the church. Obviously, Lutherans must celebrate the rediscovery of the gospel, certainty of faith, and freedom.

FCTC also mentions a third factor which must be kept in mind. Previous commemorations of the Reformation were used as opportunities for

1. *From Conflict to Communion*; hereafter *FCTC*.
2. Ibid., 9.

Lutherans to tell the story again of the beginning of the characteristic—"evangelical"—form of their church in order to justify their distinctive existence, which was tied to critique of the Roman Catholic Church. Catholics on that occasion accused Lutherans of an unjustifiable division from the true church and a rejection of the gospel of Christ.[3] But the year 2017 will see the first centennial commemoration of the Reformation to take place during the ecumenical age. It will also mark the fiftieth anniversary of the Lutheran-Catholic international dialogue. It will therefore be the first centennial commemoration to be accompanied or complemented by the extensive results of Lutheran-Catholic dialogue which have helped overcome the conflicts in faith which marked the sixteenth-century Reformation, and led to division. Those fifty years of dialogue and cooperation have created a new situation between Lutherans and Catholics.[4] For these reasons, Catholics and Lutherans therefore look to commemorate, though not celebrate, 2017 together.

A Century of Ecumenism

That this five-hundredth anniversary of the Reformation falls within an ecumenical age must be kept in view. The most significant development affecting all Christians which has happened since that sixteenth century is the development of the ecumenical movement, the movement seeking the unity of divided Christians. It encompasses at least the century starting with the 1910 World Missionary Conference at Edinburgh, Scotland in 1910, and continuing now. The ecumenical movement is a response to the major divisions in Christian history, which have taken place during past centuries and continue now, with an intention to heal those divisions. It is a response, in light of the prayer of Jesus for the unity of his disciples (John 17:21), through dialogue on issues at the root of division, through efforts to reestablish ecclesial relationships which were broken long ago, through common prayer, and through common service to humanity, and a host of other ways.

These divisions include those events in the fifth century when some ancient eastern churches could not accept the Christological language of the Councils of Ephesus (431) and Chalcedon (451), leading to separation which took place between them and the rest of the Christian world. They

3. Ibid., 5–6.
4. Ibid., 7.

include those events leading to the 1,000 year old schism between Western and Eastern Christianity, initiated by conflict in 1054 between the Sees of Rome and Constantinople, and especially by the sack of Constantinople by Western Crusaders in 1204. The Ecumenical movement is a response to the divisions in Western Christianity in the sixteenth century when conflicts at the Reformation, especially theological but also non-theological, resulted in the development of new communities separated from the traditional Church centered in the West in the See of Rome. These three great historical divisions, and others, have, for centuries, left profound scars and bitter memories on all concerned.

Stephen Charles Neill, introducing *A History of the Ecumenical Movement 1517–1948*, estimated that the reformation of the sixteenth century "did introduce divisions graver and more intractable than any which had entered in since the early days of the church."[5] "The Reformation," he said, "like all human history, is a mixed record of good and evil," and whether the good in it greatly outweighed the evil, or vice-versa, will be judged differently by members of different confessions. But, whatever be the judgment on the history as a whole, "it can hardly be denied that the divisions in the life of the Church which resulted from it were deeper and more serious than any inherited from the past. All earlier divisions had taken place within a common framework of tradition and worship. Even the more conservative forms of Protestantism represented a more radical breach with the past than anything since the Gnostic heresies."[6] If this is true, then the healing of divisions which Lutherans and Catholics seek is all the more challenging.

The ecumenical movement influenced the Second Vatican Council (1962–1965). Shortly after calling for a Council in 1959, Pope John XXIII established in 1960 a Secretariat for Promoting Christian Unity. In 1961 he also approved the invitation to other Churches and communities to send fraternal delegates to the Council, who, though not voting members, had an important influence on it, especially regarding its Decree on Ecumenism *Unitatis redintegratio*.[7] Official Lutheran observers at Vatican II sent by the

---

5. Neill, "Introduction: Division and the Search for Unity Prior to the Reformation," 23.

6. Ibid., 24.

7. Stransky, "Paul VI and the Delegated Observers/Guests to Vatican Council II," 139–46 (hereafter: *UR*).

Lutheran World Federation and the Evangelical Church of Germany were among the most consistent observers at the Council.[8]

Vatican II has also had an influence on the ecumenical movement. It gave great impetus to Catholic involvement in bilateral dialogues with many other Christian communities. The first of these, the newly established joint working group between the Catholic Church and the LWF, held its first planning meeting in August, 1965, before Vatican II ended, a second in 1966, and the dialogue itself officially began in 1967. The National Lutheran-Catholic dialogue in the USA began even earlier, with its first session held in July 1965.

It is in this ecumenical setting of newly developing Lutheran and Catholic relations, that a correspondence of a positive nature concerning the 450th anniversary of the Reformation took place in 1967. We look to see the ideas that were exchanged fifty years ago, and also how they might correspond to steps taken recently to prepare for the 500th anniversary,[9] in light of the evolution of Lutheran-Catholic relations over the last fifty years.

A Correspondence in 1967 on the 450th Anniversary of the Reformation

Cardinal Augustin Bea, President of the Secretariat for Promoting Christian Unity, wrote a letter in 1967 to the President of the Lutheran World Federation (LWF) on the occasion of the Federation's 20th anniversary and the observance of the 450th anniversary of the Reformation, to which the President, Dr. Fredrick A. Schiotz, responded. In this exchange both sides were already departing, in the spirit of the ecumenical movement, from the acrimonious behavior of the past, filled with triumphalism and/or accusations. Their exchange included positive insights which might even be useful for 2017.[10]

---

8. There were twelve Lutheran observers out of the total of 152. Only fifteen of 152 observers participated during the entire period of the four sessions of Vatican II, and three of these were Lutherans. Radano, *Lutheran and Catholic Reconciliation on Justification*, 5–6. Lutheran observers, on behalf of the Strasbourg Institute, published a volume before the fourth session began, titled *Dialogue on the Way: Protestants Report from Rome on the Vatican Council*, described as the first extended evaluation of the Vatican Council by a group of protestant observers, officially delegated by their churches to attend its sessions. Radano, 21.

9. Especially as seen in *FCTC*.

10. Both letters appear in "For the 450th Anniversary of the Reformation," 21–22.

Bea wrote that "after having spoken about this with His Holiness Pope Paul VI", he was anxious "to send greetings to you all who are soon to gather in Lund in the name of the Lutheran World Federation" to celebrate its 20th anniversary, "and . . . to observe the 450th anniversary of the Reformation." He expressed mutual regret and responsibility for the division that had taken place: "With all of you, we deeply regret that 450 years ago the unity of Western Christianity was broken. We do not wish to blame each other for this terrible schism; rather together we wish to seek ways of restoring the lost unity."

Bea recalled the recent contacts with Lutheran observers during the Council. "We still have a vivid recollection" of the LWF's participation at Vatican II through its "distinguished representatives." "For my colleagues and for me, personally, it was always a matter of joy to know that our Lutheran brethren were among us during the four sessions of the Council."

Acknowledging that only the power and counsel of God can give this unity back to us again, he also said that we are all summoned "to work at this great task in faithful obedience to our common Lord Jesus Christ." He therefore welcomed the fact that after two productive sessions of the Lutheran-Catholic working group, the theological dialogue continues, focusing on the questions concerning gospel and church: "the most important of the questions which have stood between us since the days of the Reformation are being considered." While a long road still lies ahead, "because deep-going differences continue to separate us," he expressed a trinitarian faith as the basis for hope: "We rest our hope on the love of the Father for us, the source of brotherly love of men for each other, on the prayer of Jesus Christ for his Church, and on the power of the Holy Spirit that we may be led to that unity which our Savior has desired."

Bea continued to reflect on faith. "The decisive factor for you, as for us, is faith—faith in Jesus Christ, our God and Savior, as this has been delivered to us by the Apostles and is alive in the Church." Today faith is under attack, threatened in our world as never before. Therefore, underlining the words of the report of the Lutheran-Catholic working group, he prayed that they might succeed in giving "a more effective witness to the world where so many feel incapable of faith in the Gospel of our Lord Jesus Christ or even of accepting the existence of a personal living God." Noting that Paul VI had also proclaimed this year of the 1900th anniversary of the martyrdoms of the Apostles Peter and Paul as the "Year of Faith," he

---

This publication hereafter: *IS*. The following citations are from these two pages.

expressed the hope that it may please our common Lord Jesus Christ to unite us in prayer so that the Christian faith may be strengthened and be proclaimed with new power. "Only in attending to the true message of Jesus will we find each other again." He closed sending fraternal greetings, citing 2 Corinthians 13:13.

In reply, Dr. Schiotz expressed the LWF's gratitude for Bea's cordial greetings sent on the occasion of the 450th anniversary of the Reformation and the twentieth anniversary of the LWF. He noted an effort by Lutherans to observe this anniversary somewhat differently from the past. While "we have at times been tempted to a certain triumphalism in our Reformation festivals, we pray that this temptation be thrust aside." Their churches, he said, have been encouraged "to concentrate on thanksgiving to God: gratitude for the new life He gives us through the gospel and gratitude for the call to proclaim this Gospel by word and deed in an exciting age."

Schiotz referred to a certain theology of reformation as expressed at the 1957 LWF Assembly in Minneapolis, which witnessed "to the freedom God has given us in Jesus Christ." Through all the ages "there is one holy catholic and apostolic Church, whose head is Jesus Christ. In him the Father was revealed and to him the Holy Spirit bears witness guiding us into all the truth . . . From the very beginning the Church was called to be the herald of the truth, receiving and delivering the Apostolic message of the mighty deeds of God in the history of salvation, supremely the life and earthly ministry, death and resurrection of Jesus Christ, and calling men to repentance and faith. This Apostolic tradition, in which the living Lord himself reigns and acts, remains sovereign and unchangeable throughout all ages. In every generation the church must be confronted and judged by this apostolic message. This is her ongoing reformation."

Lutheran observers at Vatican II, said Schiotz, have faithfully reported on what transpired during those historic weeks. And, "we recognize that the Holy Spirit has given us a precious unity in Jesus Christ, the Savior of all men." Lutherans would follow the discussions of the Bishops' synod then meeting in Rome, and also the dialogue of the Evangelical Lutheran-Roman Catholic Working Group.

Lutheran churches would be moved, he said, by the Cardinal's candor acknowledging "that we still have a long way to go because deep-going differences continue to separate us." He saw as an appropriate and hope-filled response to this concern from LWF churches the words from the Minneapolis Assembly: "Listening obediently to the Scriptures, abiding in the apostolic tradition" we will be free to hear what the Holy Spirit is saying to the churches in this generation. LWF member churches "will welcome participation in the "Year of Faith" proclaimed by Paul VI. Schiotz closed by focusing on faith, citing Romans 16: 25-27.

Can Their Insights Be Useful for 2017?

This unheralded exchange of letters in 1967, includes ideas still important as we look at 2017. It is interesting to recall their words in connection to the recent Lutheran–Catholic statement *From Conflict to Communion: Lutheran–Catholic Common Commemoration of the Reformation in 2017*, and in connection with fifty years of dialogue and relationship. Both letters convey new attitudes which, since then, have been confirmed over fifty years, and are ever more important as we approach 2017.

The Need for Repentance and a Healing of Memories

Bea's words suggest the need for repentance and the healing of memory. We still regret, as Bea said, that at the Reformation the unity of the Western Christianity was broken, but the reaction to that, still, is not to blame each other for that schism, but rather to seek ways of restoring the lost unity. The blame for division is shared on all sides, as the second Vatican Council acknowledged.[11] Repentance is required by all. Both Lutherans and Catholics have expressed repentance for sins against the unity of the church.[12]

On the Catholic side, for example, Pope John Paul II during the year 2000 organized a "Universal Prayer for Forgiveness" aimed at helping the Catholic Church to make an examination of conscience for sins committed during the second millennium, and make an act of repentance for them as the Church entered the third millennium. The Pope listed several categories of sins during the second millennium for which to ask God's forgiveness. One was confession of sins which have harmed the unity of the Body of Christ: "Let us pray that our recognition of the sins which have rent the unity of the body of Christ and wounded fraternal charity will facilitate the way to reconciliation and communion among all Christians."[13]

---

11. UR, 3.
12. *FCTC*, ns. 234–37.
13. "Universal Prayer for Forgiveness March 12, 2000," 53–58, here 56.

On the Lutheran side, at the LWF fifth Assembly in Evian, 1970, responding to a moving presentation by Cardinal Willebrands, who spoke positively of Luther, declared "that we as Lutheran Christians and congregations [are] prepared to acknowledge that the judgment of the Reformers upon the Roman Catholic church and its theology was not entirely free of polemical distortions, which in part have been perpetuated to the present day. We are truly sorry for the offense and misunderstanding which these polemical elements have caused our Roman Catholic brethren."[14]

In the fifty years of Lutheran-Catholic relations, we have seen that commemorating historical events has also provided opportunities contributing to building trust, healing of memories, and promoting unity. In 1980, on the occasion of the 450th anniversary of the Augsburg Confession (CA), the Lutheran-Catholic International dialogue provided the text *All Under One Christ*, 1980.[15] It recalls that the CA reflects the ecumenical purpose and catholic intention of the Reformation. "The express purpose of the Augsburg confession is to bear witness to the faith of the one, holy, catholic and apostolic church. Its concern is not with . . . the establishment of a new Church (CA VII.1), but with the preservation and renewal of the Christian faith in its purity—in harmony with the ancient church and 'the church of Rome, and in agreement with the witness of Scripture'."[16] *AUOC* admits that there are still open and unresolved problems because CA "does not adopt a position on the number of sacraments, the papacy, or on certain aspects of the episcopal order and the church's teaching office' and on other questions."[17] However reflecting on the Augsburg Confession, Catholics and Lutherans have discovered that they have "a common mind on basic doctrinal truths which points to Jesus Christ, the living center of our faith."[18] Among other things, "we are able to appeal to the Augsburg Confession when we say: Together we confess the faith in the Triune God, and the saving work of God through Jesus Christ in the Holy Spirit, which binds all Christendom together (CA I and III)."[19]

Pope Saint John Paul II during 1980, and afterwards, used this anniversary of the Augsburg Confession as an opportunity, in a number

14. Repeated in *FCTC*, 236.
15. *All Under One Christ, 1980* (hereafter: *AUOC*), 241–47.
16. Ibid., 10.
17. Ibid., 23.
18. Ibid., 17.
19. Ibid., 13.

of addresses to Catholic and Lutheran audiences in different countries, to point to the fact that Lutherans and Catholics share deep bonds of faith.[20] Commemorating this historical event by the publication and use of *AUOC* helped heal memories among Lutherans and Catholics, and call attention to the great degree of faith that they hold in common, despite continuing divisions.

In 1983, on the occasion of the 500th anniversary of Luther's birth, a number of events took place to commemorate that anniversary in a way that helped contribute to the healing of memories, and to promote unity. The Lutheran-Catholic international dialogue published in 1983 *Martin Luther: Witness to Jesus Christ*.[21] The anniversary, and this publication helped call to mind that in recent decades the study of Luther and the Reformation by Catholic scholars was putting Luther in a new and positive perspective, clearing away prejudices and misunderstanding, if not finding full mutual agreement on all of Luther's theology. Even in 1970, as already mentioned, Johannes Cardinal Willebrands, speaking at the Fifth General Assembly of the LWF gave a positive evaluation of Luther's achievements, pointing to ways in which Vatican II had dealt with concerns which Luther had articulated.[22] Following Willebrands' lead, *Witness* lists the ways in which those concerns are found in various documents of Vatican II.[23] During 1983, John Paul II and Cardinal Willebrands both spoke about Luther in sympathetic ways. The Pope in a letter to Cardinal Willebrands spoke of the "deep religious feeling" of Luther who was driven with burning passion by the question of eternal salvation."[24] He called for a twofold effort of further accurate historical work about Luther and the Reformation, and underscored the importance of the dialogue of faith in which we are engaged.[25] Willebrands, in a lecture at Leipzig, outlined extensively a number of important aspects of Luther's theology which are valuable for Catholics

---

20. Radano, *Lutheran and Catholic Reconciliation on Justification*, 68–70.

21. Luther, *Witness to Jesus Christ*. See *Growth in Agreement II Reports and Agreed Statements of Ecumenical conversations on a World level, 1982–1998* (hereafter: *GA II*), 438–42.

22. Cited in Radano, 35.

23. Luther, *Witness to Jesus Christ*, 24.

24. "Pope John Paul II's Letter on the Fifth Centenary of the Birth of Martin Luther," 83.

25. Ibid., 83–84.

and all Christians. He did not hesitate also to speak of errors and mistakes in the teachings and personal attitude of Luther.[26]

In important ways, the Lutheran-Catholic dialogue has continued to give significant attention to understanding Luther's theology and intentions. Besides *Witness*, the recent text, *From Conflict to Communion* in preparing for 2017, has a long chapter (IV) focusing on understanding Luther correctly: "Basic Themes of Martin Luther's Theology in Light of the Lutheran-Roman Catholic Dialogues."[27] This attention to understanding Luther correctly is obviously important for healing memories.

The commemoration of the 500th anniversary of the Reformation in 2017, should also be an opportunity for the healing of memory.

The Progress of Lutheran–Catholic Dialogue

In his letter, Bea urged that Instead of blaming each other for the schism that took place, we should rather, together wish to seek ways of restoring the lost unity. He therefore welcomed the progress in the early meetings, up to 1967, of the new Lutheran–Catholic dialogue. *From Conflict to Communion*, in the first of its "five ecumenical imperatives", as we prepare for 2017, says: "Catholics and Lutherans should always begin from the perspective of unity and not from the point of view of division in order to strengthen what is held in common even though the differences are more easily seen and experienced."[28]

In fact, Lutherans and Catholics can bring to 2017 the results of fifty years of international dialogue, and of many years of dialogue in the USA, in Germany and in other parts of the world.[29] Reflection on the achievements of dialogue help describe the degree of unity gained, the new relations between Lutherans and Catholics, and the degree of common identity they have begun to share. Eleven major international reports published by this international dialogue have found significant convergence/agreement concerning issues over which we have had disputes in the past, such as the

26. "Address of Cardinal Willebrands," 92–94.
27. *FCTC*, 40–79.
28. Ibid., chapter 6, 87.
29. Though we will not trace the results of these dialogues here, it can be said the insights of both international and national reports were used to foster progress, for example in developing the JDDJ. See Radano, "The Significance of the Lutheran-Catholic Dialogue," 1–8, 12–14.

relation of Gospel and Church, the Eucharist, the ministry in the church, the Church and Justification, the Apostolicity of the Church. Dialogue has shown that Lutherans and Catholics find much agreement in the faith as expressed in the Augsburg Confession. They have been able to write a joint appreciation of Martin Luther as "Witness to Jesus Christ." They have been able to write together a text preparing for a common commemoration of the Reformation in 2017. Above all, the dialogue developed the 1999 *Joint Declaration on the Doctrine of Justification* (*JDDJ*),[30] one of the landmarks of the modern ecumenical age.

The Joint Declaration on the Doctrine of Justification

The doctrine of justification "was of central importance for the Lutheran reformation of the sixteenth century" and "the crux of all the disputes."[31] With the *JDDJ* Lutherans and Catholics can claim now that "a consensus in basic truths of the doctrine of justification exists between Lutherans and Catholics."[32] And "the doctrinal condemnations of the sixteenth century, insofar as they relate to the doctrine of justification, appear in a new light. The teaching of the Lutheran churches presented in this declaration does not fall under the condemnations from the Council of Trent. The condemnations in the Lutheran Confessions do not apply to the teaching of the Roman Catholic Church presented in this declaration."[33]

The *JDDJ* is one of the milestones of the ecumenical movement. In 2006, the Methodist World Council, after an internal process, and in collaboration with the two original signers, officially joined them in accepting the *JDDJ*. Studies have shown that other Christian World Communions, in dialogue with the Catholic Church, have produced statements on justification which show many similarities with the presentation of the *JDDJ*.[34]

This land mark text on justification has changed relationships between Lutherans and Catholics, and has broad implications. One major theological implication of this, according to Walter Kasper, is that the *JDDJ* was able to clarify other differences from the sixteenth century. "With the JDDJ," he

---

30. Found in *GA II*, 566–82.
31. *JDDJ*, 1 in *GA II*.
32. Ibid., 40.
33. Ibid., 41.
34. Kasper, *Harvesting the Fruits*, 21. It speaks here of the Anglican Catholic and the Reformed-Catholic international dialogues.

said, "it was possible to see anew that the affirmation of *sola gratia* and *sola fide* does not contradict the affirmation that by grace we are made capable of bearing good fruits through works of justice, mercy and active love."[35] In another perspective, as Ishmael Noko, former General Secretary of the Lutheran World Federation, and signer of the *JDDJ* reminds us, the conflict at the time of the Reformation not only affected the church, but society at large. The theological, ecclesial, and social divisions created in Europe during the Reformation were exported to the rest of the world through colonization, immigration and missionary activities. Therefore, "the signing of the *Joint Declaration* has helped to close a chapter of conflict and division in Europe and the world. One of the most important messages of the *Joint Declaration* is that, wherever in the world they may live, Lutherans and Roman Catholics are not enemies anymore but sisters and brothers in Christ."[36]

Many Other Results of Dialogue

Besides this great achievement, the dialogue has shown that Lutherans and Catholics had never been totally separated in faith. According to *All Under One Christ*, in regard to faith in the Triune God, "Through all the disputes and differences of the sixteenth century, Lutheran and Catholic Christians remained one in this central and most important truth of the Christian faith."[37] In the profound bitterness created in the sixteenth century, there were still degrees of communion which they shared, and could build on once dialogue became possible.

The dialogue has continued to explore those matters in which they have had conflict. Today, there is significant effort to study and acknowledge the achievements of dialogue reports, as was done in a special way with justification. Cardinal Walter Kasper, with The Pontifical Council for Promoting Christian Unity, examined in 2009 the reports of four International dialogues in which the Catholic Church has been involved: those with Lutherans, Anglicans, Reformed and Methodists.[38] This was the first time that the dialogue reports of four different international bilaterals

---

35. Kaspar, *Harvesting the Fruits*, 103.

36. Rev. Dr. Ishmael Noko, General Secretary, Lutheran World Federation, foreword in Radano, *Lutheran and Catholic Reconciliation*, xvii.

37. *AUOC*, 13.

38. See Kaspar, *Harvesting the Fruits*.

were explored together, by one of the sponsors, in consultation with the other sponsors. The study examined all of their reports produced up until then, together, approximately forty, in four areas: (1) fundamentals of our common faith: Jesus Christ and the Holy Trinity, (2) salvation, justification sanctification, (3) the Church, and (4) the sacraments of baptism and Eucharist. It found a great deal of convergence/agreement on these questions in the Lutheran and Catholic dialogue, but, multilaterally between that dialogue and the three others.

Harvesting draws "some preliminary conclusions" from this study. "It can happily be stated that some of the classic disputes, which were at the root of our painful divisions, have today been basically resolved through a new consensus on fundamental points of doctrine."[39] We have discovered that in common we share the Gospel as the Word of God and the Good News for all humanity, and we share the Creeds of the first centuries which summarize the Gospel message and give an authentic interpretation of it. We confess together the Triune God, and that Jesus Christ our common Lord and savior is truly human and truly divine, the one and universal mediator between God and man."[40] We have discovered "a fresh and renewed understanding of the relation between Scripture and Tradition", so that today "it is no longer possible to set Scripture and Tradition at odds with each other." For all of us, Scripture is the witness to the original and primeval normative apostolic Tradition, given once and for all times."[41] There is basic agreement on the doctrine of justification. The core message of the Bible "is God's gracious and merciful salvific will to reconcile sinful humanity with him and to bring reconciliation and peace (*shalom*) to our divided and chaotic world . . . This is the meaning of the doctrine of justification."[42] There is a deepened understanding of the nature of the church, a re-emphasis on the Trinitarian roots of the church, and a focus on the nature of the church as *koinonia*/communion. In regard to sharply contrasting visions of the Church seen in the past, that of a visible institutional church in contrast to a hidden, spiritual church, or a Church as *Mater et Magistra* in contrast to a Church under the gospel, or, a Church as sacrament of grace, in contrast to a Church as *creatura verbi*, "many elements of convergence have been

---

39. Ibid., 100.
40. Ibid., 101.
41. Ibid., 102.
42. Ibid., 103.

found in these and other controversies."[43] There are new approaches to the sacraments of baptism and Eucharist. The rediscovery of our common baptism has helped Catholics and other Christians to recognize each other again as brothers and sisters in Christ.[44]

There are many other convergences that could be mentioned from this study. At the same time the study shows that in every area there is more work to be done. "It must be acknowledged honestly and realistically that although our dialogues have brought progress, they have not yet led us to the final goal of full visible communion." Thus, according to Kasper, the churches find themselves "at an intermediate stage"[45] with much work still to do. Furthermore, another recent study of reports of Lutheran-Catholic dialogue, international, regional and national, entitled *Declaration on the Way: Church, Ministry and Eucharist* (2016) identified and documented 32 agreements on these three topics, and ten remaining differences still to be resolved. All of these point to the progress that Lutherans and Catholics have made in resolving issues which contributed to their separation in the sixteenth century.

Commemorating the Five-Hundredth Anniversary of the Reformation in an Ecumenical Age

Lutheran and Catholic relationships were significantly changed at Vatican II. Both Bea and Schiotz recognized this. Bea began with a "vivid recollection" of the participation of LWF representatives at Vatican II and the care with which they participated during four sessions of the Council. Their participation amounted to "a new fellowship among us, which was made possible by the power of the Holy Spirit, (which) has not diminished since the end of the Council but has grown in dialogue and in cooperation." According to Schiotz, what the Lutheran observers reported about the Council "has warmed our hearts. We recognize that the Holy Spirit has given us a precious unity in Jesus Christ, the Savior of all men."

---

43. Ibid., 104.
44. Ibid., 105.
45. Ibid., 106.

"The Struggle of the Sixteenth Century Is Over"

The Lutheran-Catholic dialogue, of course, is not finished. Important issues still need to be resolved. Still, looking toward 2017, *From Conflict to Communion* could also say, in a similar way, after decades of dialogue convergences and agreements had been found on many issues, that "Catholics and Lutherans realize that they and the communities in which they live out their faith belong to the one body of Christ." Thus, "the awareness is dawning on Lutherans and Catholics that the struggle of the sixteenth century is over. The reasons for mutually condemning each other's faith have fallen by the wayside."[46] *FCTC*'s second ecumenical imperative could say that "Lutherans and Catholics must let themselves continually be transformed by the encounter with the other and by the mutual witness of faith."[47] Their separate identities were created in division. Dialogue results show that they are moving towards developing a common identity as Christians who can serve the mission of Christ together.

In the historical context of the sixteenth century in which the Reformation took place, civic authorities, whether emperors, kings or princes, had some influence on Christian leaders, contributing at times to making dialogue on decisive theological issues very difficult. While the theological conflicts were decisive, that historical context influenced the division with which Christians were left by mid-century, and for centuries afterwards. Today, in a different historical context, the ecumenical age fosters dialogue between the churches, and they are no longer influenced in that dialogue by civic authorities as they were in the sixteenth century.

Giving Common Witness to God's Mercy

In his letter to the LWF in 1967, Cardinal Bea focused on the "decisive factor" of faith, and even though the new relationship between Lutherans and Catholics was still a fledgling relationship, he called for common witness to this faith. He focused on "faith in Jesus Christ, our God and Savior, as delivered to us by the Apostles, because faith is under attack today, as never before—a faith under attack." Bea appealed for common witness by underlining the words of a report of the still fledging Lutheran-Catholic Joint Working Group, praying "that together we might succeed in giving 'a

---

46. *FCTC*, 238.
47. Ibid., 240–41.

more effective witness to the world where so many feel incapable of faith in the gospel of our Lord Jesus Christ or even accepting the existence of a personal living God.'" Bea called for common prayer. As Paul VI has proclaimed this year of the 1900th anniversary of the martyrdom of the apostles Peter and Paul as the "Year of Faith," Bea appealed that Christ "unite us in prayer so that the Christian faith may be strengthened and be proclaimed with new power. Only in attending to the true message of Jesus will we find each other again."

In preparations for 2017, the "fifth imperative" of *From Conflict to Communion* is that "Catholics and Lutherans should witness together to the mercy of God in proclamation and service to the world." How appropriate this is from both Lutheran and Catholic points of view. The current "year of mercy" as designated by Pope Francis for Catholics, began in December, 2015, and extends to December 2016, overlapping as it were, the beginning of the year of commemoration of the 500th anniversary of the Reformation which begins October 31, 2016. Cardinal Willebrands in his address in Leipzig in 1983, commemorating the 500th anniversary of Luther's birth, recalled that among Luther's main concerns were the basic power of evil, the impotence of man, and the all-pervading might of God. Because of Luther's way of pursuing these concerns, he can be seen, according to Willebrands, "as the spokesman of man, who—mortal and turned inwards onto himself—can rely on nothing other than God's mercy."[48] On this basis Willebrands in 1983, like Bea before him in 1967, and *FCTC* after him in 2013, called for common witness, in a way that resounds even more on the eve of 2017: "I ask whether the time is not more than ripe for us to join hands in trying to see to what extent, face to face with this world of ours, we can today bear a joint witness to the good news of our redemption, the message that the Church is intended to serve. Ought we not, driven on by the memory of history and guilt, jointly to mold and shape our present?"[49] Lutherans and Catholics share deep bonds of unity in faith, enabling them now, to begin joint witness to the good news of our redemption, the message that the church is intended to serve. On this 500th anniversary of the Reformation, would this not honor those on both sides of the struggle in the sixteenth century who took positions, in good conscience, out of deep conviction for the good of the Church, even though they were in conflict?

48. "Address of Cardinal Willebrands," 92–94; cited in Radano, *Lutheran and Catholic Reconciliation*, 72–73.

49. Ibid., 73.

The Hope for Unity

An authentic commemoration of the 500th anniversary of the Reformation in this ecumenical age can no longer just look to the past. It must also look forward to the future. Lutherans and Catholics can commemorate together this anniversary, but not celebrate it because they are still divided. As Bea indicated, "a long road still lies ahead, because deep seated differences continue to separate us." But we place our trust in God: "we rest our hope on the love of the Father for us, . . . on the prayer of Jesus Christ for his Church, and on the power of the Holy Spirit that we may be led to that unity which our Savior has desired. Schiotz, responded in the words of the 1957 Minneapolis Assembly, that "Listening obediently to the Scriptures, abiding in the apostolic tradition," we will be free to hear what the Holy Spirit is saying to the churches in this generation.

In 2017, as Lutherans and Catholics commemorate the 500th anniversary of the Reformation still divided, they can also celebrate the great strides already taken to restore unity between them. They can celebrate together the ecumenical movement for unity, to which Lutherans and Catholics both contribute. They can celebrate the historic achievement of the *Joint Declaration on the Doctrine of Justification,* and common perspectives already reached on many other matters of faith, their ability to undertake common witness to the gospel. They can and must also look forward to the day when, in obedience to the will of Christ (John 17:21), they will be able to celebrate together their unity as disciples of the one Shepherd, Jesus Christ.

The Lutheran-Catholic Statement *Martin Luther—Witness to Jesus Christ* (1983) outlines "Luther's legacy and our common task."[50] Of the nine areas concerning which, it is said, "it is possible for us today to learn from Luther together," two seem especially appropriate on this anniversary which comes in an ecumenical age:

> He testifies that God's forgiveness is the only basis and hope for human life.
>
> He exhorts us to remember that reconciliation and Christian community can only exist where not only "the rule of faith" is followed, but also the "rule of love", "which always thinks well of everyone, is not suspicious, believes the best about its neighbors and calls anyone who is baptized a saint" (Martin Luther).[51]

50. *Witness to Christ,* V.
51. *Witness to Christ,* 26.

Bibliography

"All Under One Christ, 1980. Statement on the Augsburg Confession by the Roman Catholic/Lutheran Joint Commission." In *Growth in Agreement: Reports and Agreed Statements of Ecumenical Conversations on a World Level*, edited by Harding Meyer and Lukas Vischer. New York: Paulist, 1984.

"For the 450th Anniversary of the Reformation." The *Secretariat for Promoting Christian Unity Vatican City Information Service* 3 (1967) 21–22.

From Conflict to Communion: Lutheran–Catholic Common Commemoration of the Reformation in 2017. Report of the Lutheran–Roman Catholic Commission on Unity. Leipzig: Evangelishe Verlagsanstalt Bonifatius, 2013.

Gros, Jeffrey, et al. "Martin Luther-Witness to Jesus Christ, 1983." In *Growth in Agreement: Reports and Agreed Statements of Ecumenical conversations on a World level, 1982-1998*. Geneva: World Council of Churches; and Grand Rapids: Eerdmans, 2000.

Kasper, Walter. *Harvesting the Fruits: Aspects of Christian Faith in Ecumenical Dialogue.* London: Continuum, 2009.

Neill, Stephen Charles. *A History of the Ecumenical Movement 1517–1948.* Edited by Routh Rouse and Stephen Charles Neill. 2nd ed. Philadelphia: Westminster, 1967.

Radano, John A. *Lutheran and Catholic Reconciliation on Justification: A Chronology of the Holy See's Contributions, 1961–1999, to New Relationships between Lutherans and Catholics and to Steps Leading to the Joint Declaration on the Doctrine of Justification.* Grand Rapids: Eerdmans, 2009.

———. "The Significance of the Lutheran–Catholic Dialogue in the United States: After Fifty Years." *Ecumenical Trends* (October, 2015) 1–8, 12–14.

Stransky, Thomas F. "Paul VI and the Delegated Observers/Guests to Vatican Council II." *Paolo VI e ecumenismo.* Rome: Istituto Paolo VI, 2001.

Preface

Remembering Luther: A Reformer in Church History

—Christopher M. Bellitto

REMEMBERING IS AN ACT of creating identity. For church historians doing an honest job of their craft, remembering does not mean declaring winners and losers. That is too often the task of apologists masquerading as church historians. They take proof texts they like from the historical record and sweep uncomfortable pieces undercutting their position into the dusty corners. An honest historian assesses people in their own contexts and places them on a wider canvas, finding all of history instructive whether it is consoling or unsettling. Remembering Luther as a reformer is a step toward identifying all of church history as reform history however messy it may be (and it is).

As the church catholic—as Philip Krey neatly puts it in his essay—commemorates the age of reformations, it is insightful to discover how people between 1517 and today remembered Luther and his legacy. The contributions to this volume nimbly walk us through this shared history, often thanks to a digital humanities *tour-de-force*. Let us proceed on that walk with the words of the eminent papal historian Eamon Duffy in mind.

> I think it is the historian's job to tell the truth and if the truth goes against the church then so be it. It is more important to tell the truth than to protect the church . . . I think historians have the

great responsibility of bringing home to the church that it is a historical community made up of fallible people and that therefore the past of the church is not a sacred area . . . It is very important that if the church goes to the past, then it should be the real past it goes to and not some fantasy or some heritage past that has been manicured and tidied up.[1]

For some Catholics of a certain stripe, remembering Luther reflects an attitude I once heard among Catholic seminarians studying for the priesthood. Very few had signed up for a seminar on the ecumenical movement from one of the field's leaders. "Why not?," this visiting professor was asked. "Because for these young priests-in-training," he explained, "ecumenism means 'we're right, you're wrong, come back.'" That attitude brings to mind Pope Pius IX's hedged invitation in advance of Vatican I (1869–1870). The pope sent word of the general council's convocation to Protestant representatives and some Orthodox patriarchs suggesting that this would be a good time for them to return to unity with the Catholic Church under his authority. Not surprisingly, they declined.

Many, perhaps most Catholics would be riled even after fifty years of ecumenical progress and a very fruitful Lutheran-Catholic dialogue in particular to hear (let alone accept) the statement, "Luther was a good Catholic."[2] The positive attitude behind that statement reflects a scholarly sea-change, of course. That same seminary for years had a church history course where the teacher approached the Reformation this way. "Martin Luther was a very bad man," this priest-professor said before turning his yellowed pages to declare with satisfaction, "Now, the Council of Trent."

Even today, use the word *reform* in church settings and most think only of Luther or Vatican II, which is why we must reiterate that the only constant in church history is change. Neither *change* nor *reform* are four-letter words. Studying the idea of reform in and of itself (as opposed to "The Reformation") has been with us for over a half-century. It was the great intellectual historian Gerhart Ladner who, just a few years before Vatican II's opening in 1962 as it turned out, published *The Idea of Reform: Its Impact on Christian Thought and Action in the Age of the Fathers*.[3]

---

1. Quoted in *Commonweal*, January 14, 2000.

2. On Luther's Catholic context and especially his personal devotions and spirituality, see most recently Krey and Krey, eds., *The Catholic Luther*, and also Hendrix, *Martin Luther*. For a history, reflection, and analysis on the dialogue co-authored by a Catholic and a Lutheran, see Wood and Wengert, *A Shared Spiritual Journey*.

3. Ladner, *The Idea of Reform*. For an evaluation of Ladner's impact, see the articles

About a decade before, Ladner's historical approach to reform had been explored theologically by the French Dominican Yves Congar in his *Vraie et fausse réforme dans l'Église*.⁴ For our period, the German priest Hubert Jedin broke down the polemical approach to the reformation era by demonstrating how Luther's critiques were mainstream and in continuity with longstanding late medieval calls for reform.⁵ In our own time, no one on the Catholic side has done more to professionalize church history nor to help us understand that ecumenical sea-change among historians of reform than the Jesuit John O'Malley.⁶

Moving more properly to Luther's 1517 stance and this volume's *terminus a quo*, we should note that the exasperation of this monk from a reformed Augustinian house was not original nor were the problems he pointed out new. It was the late medieval church hierarchy itself that continually postponed the needed reform in head and members (*reformatio in capite et in membris*) for two centuries because of greed, in-fighting, and a power struggle with conciliarists arguing that a general council and not the papacy was the highest church authority. The fourteenth-century Avignon papacy spent most of its time turned in on its curial self. The Great Western Schism followed with two papacies (each pope with his own college of cardinals, loyal bishops and curia, and political support) from 1378 to 1409 and then a third until 1417—nearly four decades where unity was nowhere to be found. So confused and fearful was one Toledo bishop that he prayed at Mass *pro illo qui est verus papa*: loosely translated, "for the true pope,

---

by three of his doctoral students, Lester L. Field Jr., et al., comprising Part I of *Reassessing Reform*, 17–57.

4. Congar, *Vraie et fausse réforme dans l'Église*, 2nd ed; now available via Paul Philibert, trans. *True and False Reform in the Church*. Note that in the first (1950) edition of *Vraie et fausse réforme*, Congar did not take much of an ecumenical stance toward Protestants, but ill health and a burdensome schedule prevented him from revising that treatment for the 1968 edition; this part is not translated in the 2010 edition (on these points, see the 2010 translation, xv and 3). Nevertheless, Congar directly considered this volume's focus in his "Church Reform and Luther's Reformation, 1517–1967," *Lutheran World*, 351–59.

5. Jedin, *Geschichte des Konzils von Trient*, 4 vols. in 5; the first two volumes are available in English: Ernest Graf, trans. *A History of the Council of Trent*. For an appreciation of Jedin's contribution to reorienting Catholic scholarship toward the reformation era, see Alberigo, "Réforme en tant que critère de l'histoire d l'Église," 72–81.

6. For a survey, see most recently O'Malley, "Catholic Church History," 1–26, but on these points especially 2–5, 12, 18–19. On changing positions toward Trent and Vatican II specifically, see O'Malley, *Trent: What Happened at the Council?*, 10–12, and more broadly his *What Happened at Vatican II?*, 15–52.

whichever one he is." We laugh because it's funny. It was also sad because the confusion and uncertainty were all too true.

We also laugh with clear-eyed hindsight at the Medici Pope Leo X's dismissal of Luther as a quarrelsome German monk stirring up some local trouble. Yet Pope Adrian VI who followed him saw that even though Leo had excommunicated Luther just a year before, there may still have been a window for Catholics and Luther's followers to find common ground (though admittedly the pope was trying to get German princes to join Rome in opposing Luther). A student of none other than Erasmus, Adrian sent his legate named Francesco Chieregati to the Diet of Nuremberg with instructions to admit church errors:

> [Y]ou will promise that we will expend every effort to reform first this curia, whence perhaps all this evil has come, so that, as corruption spread from that place to every lower place, the good health and reformation of all may also issue forth. We consider ourselves all the more bound to attend to this, the more we perceive the entire world longing for such a reformation.

There is a lesson here about the pace of change. Both Luther and Adrian agreed that slower is better when it came to implementing reform. Writing within months of each other, Luther and Adrian cautioned against doing too much too quickly. To his legate, Adrian recommended reforms that were slow and not sudden "lest in a desire to reform everything at the same time we throw everything into confusion," the pope told Chieregati. "He who scrubs too much draws blood."[7] Luther had a bigger problem on his hands: not long after he took a turn from critiquing to resisting, he was accused by those also disposed to reform of not going far and fast enough. During Christmas season 1521, Andreas Karlstadt led his followers in putting church reform into high gear. Luther was as surprised as some of his congregants to find Karlstadt pushing for vernacular Masses celebrated without vestments, for receiving communion under both bread and wine and without fasting, for priests getting married in a high-profile ceremony, and for destroying images and organs. If a ritual, devotion, or object smacked of Roman Catholicism, it was fair game.

Luther was an impatient and stubborn man, it is true, but even these changes went too far and too quickly for him. In response, Luther preached eight often-overlooked sermons in Wittenberg known as the *Invocavit*

---

7. Olin, ed., *The Catholic Reformation*, 122–27.

sermons because he began on the first Sunday of Lent in March 1522.[8] Change should be grounded in gospel precedents and love. They should be instituted gradually and explained clearly so they would be understood and embraced for the right reasons. Luther himself used an immediately recognizable image (referring also to 1 Cor 3:2) to make his case:

> Dear brother, if you have suckled long enough, do not at once cut off the breast, but let your brother be suckled as you were suckled. I would not have gone so far as you have done, if I had been here. The cause is good, but there has been too much haste.

Luther was clear: he agreed with those in Wittenberg disavowing the Roman Catholic sacrifice of the Mass. Take it away suddenly and by force, however, and people couldn't decide for themselves what they believed.

> [I]t should be preached and taught with tongue and pen that to hold Mass in [the Roman Catholic] manner is sinful, and yet no one should be dragged away from it by the hair . . .
> Now if I should rush in and abolish it by force, there are many who would be compelled to consent to it and yet not know where they stand, whether it is right or wrong, and they would say. I do not know if it is right or wrong, I do not know where I stand, I was compelled by force to submit to the majority. And this forcing and commanding results in a mere mockery, an external show, a fool's play, man-made ordinances, sham saints, and hypocrites. For where the heart is not good, I care nothing at all for the work. We must first win the hearts of the people . . .
> In short, I will preach it, teach it, write it, but I will constrain no man by force, for faith must come freely without compulsion. Take myself as an example. I opposed indulgences and all the papists, but never with force.

Modern Catholics failed to learn Luther's lesson. A great irony in the history of church reform is that many Catholics fired up by Vatican II (1962–1965) went quite far quite fast without knowing why changes were being made or explaining them to parishes. Why was it not permitted to eat meat on Fridays for so many centuries but a week later it was just fine? Why was the priest now facing the congregation during Mass, praying and preaching in the common language of the local people, and inviting many more laypeople to serve on the altar as lectors? What happened to organ music and traditional architecture? For some, this was exciting; for

---

8. Pelikan and Lehmann, eds., *Luther's Works*, 51:70-100.

others, the changes were dizzying and confusing. The inevitable revolutionary swing too far one way led to an opposing pendulum swing blow-back reaction the other way. It appears Catholicism is coming to something of a Hegelian synthesis of what worked and what didn't now that more than a half-century has passed since Vatican II adjourned in 1965. History demonstrates it takes at least that long for the church to receive, to interpret, to implement, and most importantly to balance a general council's teachings.[9]

To return to Luther's *Invocavit* sermons, we see there a key point that he believed Karlstadt and others were missing: changing externals without an essential internal *metanoia* was just moving furniture around a beat-up house. Luther feared, to repeat his words, "a mere mockery, an external show, a fool's play, man-made ordinances, sham saints, and hypocrites." As Ladner pointed out in *The Idea of Reform*, for a thousand years there was no concept of institutional reform because there was no institution as we think of it to reform. The patristic idea of reform is personal reform. Simony and its partners pluralism and absenteeism emerged as problems but they were grounded in greed. The structural change of buying and selling offices needed to be changed, surely, but it was the vice underneath the structure that was the fundamental problem. Clean out the vice and the problem dwindles. Change the structure without rooting out the vice, on the other hand, and sin just finds another outlet to flourish.

This pivot to personal reform as the *sine qua non* of true reform is often lost when we discuss Luther, Vatican II, or any other moment in church history. Inner change is far more crucial than outer change, which is why breaking statues for the sake of destruction is just an iconoclastic temper tantrum. It would be a new type of fanaticism or arithmetical piety—and it was just that type of mindless devotion that reformers like Erasmus and Luther had been criticizing in the first place. What needs to occur first is an attitude adjustment. As Pope Francis put it an interview a few months after his election in March 2013, "The structural and organizational reforms are secondary—that is, they come afterward. The first reform must be the attitude."[10] Without a change of heart, which is the very essence of personal reform, even the most well-thought-out plans for structural reform will not

---

9. For an analysis of fifty years of competing interpretations and implementations of this council, see Faggioli, *Vatican II*.

10. "A Big Heart Open to God," interview with Antonio Spadaro, *America*, September 30, 2013.

take root. That is the most important lesson in remembering church history as the history of reform.

Bibliography

Alberigo, Giuseppe. "Réforme en tant que critère de l'histoire d l'Église." *Revue d'histoire ecclésiastique* 76 (1981) 72–81.
Congar, Ives. *Vraie et fausse réforme dans l'Église*. 2nd ed. Paris: Cerf, 1968. ET= *True and False Reform in the Church*. Translated by Paul Philibert. Collegeville, MN: Liturgical, 2010.
Faggioli, Massimo. *Vatican II: The Battle for Meaning*. Mahwah NJ: Paulist, 2012.
Field, Lester L. Jr., et al. *Reassessing Reform: A Historical Investigation into Church Renewal*, edited by Christopher M. Bellitto and David Zachariah Flanagin. Part 1, 17–57. Washington, DC: Catholic University of America Press, 2012.
Hendrix, Scott. *Martin Luther: Visionary Reformer*. New Haven: Yale University Press, 2015.
Jedin, Hubert. *Geschichte des Konzils von Trient*. 4 vols. in 5. Freiburg: Herder, 1949–1975. The first two volumes are available in English: *A History of the Council of Trent*. Translated by Ernest Graf. London: Nelson, 1957–1961.
Krey, Philip D. W., and Peter D. S. Krey, eds. *The Catholic Luther: His Early Writings* Mahwah, NJ: Paulist, 2016.
Ladner, Gerhart B. *The Idea of Reform: Its Impact on Christian Thought and Action in the Age of the Fathers*. Cambridge: Harvard University Press, 1959.
Olin, John W., ed. *The Catholic Reformation: Savonarola to Ignatius Loyola*. New York: Fordham University Press, 1992
O'Malley, John W. "Catholic Church History: One Hundred Years of the Discipline." *Catholic Historical Review* 101 (2015) 1–26.
———. *Trent: What Happened at the Council?* Cambridge, MA: Belknap, 2013.
———. *What Happened at Vatican II?* Cambridge, MA: Belknap, 2008.
Pelikan, Jaroslav, and Helmut T. Lehmann, eds. *Luther's Works*, 55 vols. Philadelphia: Muhlenberg, 1955–1986. 51:70–100.
Wood, Susan K., and Timothy J. Wengert. *A Shared Spiritual Journey: Lutherans and Catholics Travel toward Unity*. Mahwah, NJ: Paulist, 2016.

Acknowledgments

It is with great thanks that I acknowledge the role of William Rusch and Norman Hjelm in the conception of this volume. Their suggestions for contributors and sources and their editorial comments have been most helpful in completing this volume. I am also most grateful for the patience of the contributors to the volume on the road to publication. This volume was originally part of a series Reformation Resources and found a home with Cascade Books. Therefore I am most grateful to K. C. Hanson and MatthewWimmer and the staff at Wipf and Stock Publishers for their help in bringing this book to print. I am also grateful to John Radano and Christopher Bellitto, whose contributions have put the essays in the context of the history of ecumenism since the Reformation.

I am also grateful to the Lutheran Theological Seminary at Philadelphia and the sabbatical it granted me to do the research for and compile this volume.

Abbreviations

AUOC   "All Under One Christ, 1980: Statement on the Augsburg Confession by the Roman Catholic/Lutheran Joint Commission." In *Growth in Agreement: Reports and Agreed Statements of Ecumenical Conversations on a World Level*. Edited by Harding Meyer and Lukas Vischer. New York: Paulist, 1984

FCTC   *From Conflict to Communion: Lutheran–Catholic Common Commemoration of the Reformation in 2017. Report of the Lutheran–Roman Catholic Commission on Unity*. Leipzig: Evangelishe Verlagsanstalt Bonifatius, 2013

GA II   Gros, Jeffrey, Harding Meyer, and Willima G. Rusch. "Martin Luther—Witness to Jesus Christ, 1983." In *Growth in Agreement: Reports and Agreed Statements of Ecumenical conversations on a World Level, 1982–1998*. Grand Rapids: Eerdmans, 2000

IS   The *Secretariat for Promoting Christian Unity Vatican City Information Service* 3 (1967)

JDDJ   John A. Radano. *Lutheran and Catholic Reconciliation on Justification: A Chronology of the Holy See's Contributions, 1961-1999, to New Relationships between Lutherans and Catholics and to Steps Leading to the Joint Declaration on the Doctrine of Justification*. Grand Rapids: Eerdmans, 2009

ABBREVIATIONS

LW Martin Luther, *Luther's Works*. Edited by Jaroslav Pelikan and Helmut T. Lehmann. 55 vols. Philadelphia: Muhlenberg; St. Louis: Concordia, 1955–1986

UR Thomas F. Stransky, "Paul VI and the Delegated Observers/Guests to Vatican Council II." In *Paolo VI e ecumenismo*. Rome: Istituto Paolo VI, 2001

WA *D. Martin Luthers Werke, Kritisch Gesamtausgabe: [Schriften]*. 73 vols. Weimar: Böhlaus, 1883–2009

WABr *D. Martin Luthers Werke, Kritische Gesamtausgabe: Briefwechsel*. 18 vols. Weimar: Böhlaus, 1930–1983

Introduction

—Philip D. Krey

Despite its long tradition of reform, The Roman Catholic Church was unable to reform itself in head and members in the late middle ages. The rejection by the papacy and church of Martin Luther's proposals for reform in the Ninety-Five Theses in 1517, his refusal to recant at the Diet of Worms in 1521, and the subsequent rejection by the church of the proposals to the church catholic by the Lutheran movement at the Diet of Augsburg in 1530 hurtled the church towards schism. The Roman Catholic Church was beset with further divisions with the Reformed traditions spawned by Ulrich Zwingli and John Calvin in Switzerland and France, with subsequent splintering in the Radical Reformation, and with the Anglican tradition in the English Reformation. These reformation traditions were also not able to remain in communion with each other over the centuries and differed publicly on many issues of doctrine, ministry, and the Christian life. The question asked the essayists in this volume from the Lutheran, Anglican, Reformed, and Roman Catholic traditions was how over five hundred years each tradition observed or did not observe the Lutheran Reformation that began on October 31, 1517.

As the five hundredth anniversary of Luther's nailing of the Ninety-Five Theses approaches more than a century of ecumenical progress among these divided churches has achieved greater theological agreement and practical cooperation towards the goal of restoring visible unity in Christ. Pronounced a heretic in the sixteenth century, in the last fifty years the person and theology of Martin Luther and the teachings of The Augsburg Confession have been recognized both by Roman Catholic scholarship and the Papacy to be within the bounds of a reform of Roman Catholic Theology. The Anglican and Lutheran churches which coexisted alongside each other for centuries sharing common roots but largely ignoring each other's commemorations and observances of the Reformation are now in full communion in many parts of the world and can celebrate the five hundredth anniversary of the Reformation together. Similarly many Reformed traditions and most Lutheran traditions have agreed to be in full communion and relate in a spirit of mutual affirmation and admonition. The inertia of five hundred years of division will not be overcome quickly, but these essays will show that the Holy Spirit is moving the arc of history towards Jesus' prayer that the church will be one.

In the first essay in this volume, "Martin Luther and the Lutheran Reformation—From a Doctor of the Church Attempting to Reform Catholic Theology in 1517 to *doctor communis* of the Church in 2017," I have traced this transformation of Luther and the movement he spawned from a heretical threat to the unity of the church to a resource for renewal in the church catholic. In the Ninety-Five Theses the young Augustinian monk and professor, a teacher of the church, attempted to reform a pastoral care practice of selling indulgences. Rebuffed and excommunicated then, five hundred years later he serves as the "common doctor." As the movement spawned by Luther's "nailing" of the Ninety-Five Theses on the door of the Castle Church arrived at its first centennial in October 31, 1617, the event was celebrated to cement the movement's confessional identity and integrity in a hostile environment. Before then and in the following century the date was hardly regularly observed. The significant dates in Luther's biography were celebrated which still continues and the key dates when various territories adopted the Reformation. The celebrations of 1817, however, marked a major transition in the anniversary observances.

The first two centennial commemorations focused on Lutheran confessional identity and its message of justification by grace through faith and it corollaries. The 1817 commemoration was one in which the commemoration was a celebration of Lutheran identification with Protestant themes of liberalism, freedom, and progress that were attributed to Luther. The twentieth century sobered observances given two world wars and the holocaust in the land of Lutheranism's birth, but signs of reconciliation appeared in the ecumenical movement. Throughout the essay, when relevant,

I noted important commemorations of Luther's birth, death etc. as Luther the "prophet, teacher and hero" took on equal importance with the movement he launched. As grist for my historian's mill, I shared a number of mini-stories to shape the larger story of Luther from heretic to common teacher and the Lutheran commemorations from protesting movement to a world communion that flirted with protestant triumphalism in the nineteenth century only to have its course corrected by history and Luther's own theological values of tradition and catholicity in the twentieth.

The essay includes documents and references both to popular, artistic, official, ecclesial, and media sources to demonstrate how the observances have changed from a spirit of rivalry and acrimony to collaboration for church reform. To tell the story of the commemorations I have used sermons, broadsheets, posters, newspaper and magazine articles, podcasts of museum descriptions, tourism brochures and collateral, hymns and hymnals, Bach cantatas, ecumenical statements as well as historical documents, and texts. The 500th anniversary plans have brought the commemorations full circle as they will not be just Lutheran or German but ecumenical and global. They will not be over against one another but a collaborative event among the various communions. This is the theme of all the essays in the volume.

The essayists were given latitude to narrate the five-hundred-year history of observances in relation to the significant anniversaries using only those dates that were significant for their traditions. Since commemorations of October 31, 1517, have been almost nonexistent in the history of Anglicanism rather than trace anniversary celebrations in the years of 1517, 1617, 1717, 1817, 1917, and 2017, Robert W. Prichard uses those years as symbolic markers to trace the often close relationship of Anglicans and Lutherans. The essay, "Martin Luther and the Episcopal Church," points to "both high and low points in that relationship and ponders the question as to why Anglicans have not been more active in their celebration of relationship to and indebtedness to the Lutheran churches."

Prichard argues that while the Lutheran Reformation had a significant impact on the early development of Anglican theology and the Anglican Church its influence was not highlighted until the nineteenth century. Using multiple documentary and digital historical sources Prichard traces the long "shared history" of the Lutheran and Anglican traditions that had strong intersections at the beginning, but personalities and events led to the formation of two distinct traditions whose paths crossed through royal marriage, in the mission field, especially in India and the Mideast, and in the colonial parishes in America in which Lutheran congregations lacking qualified clergy called Anglian priests to serve them. There was an eighteenth-century attempt at Protestant Union between King George I of England and Frederick William I of Prussia, but fear of Prussian expansion poured cold water on ecumenical partnerships for a century and a half.

In Prichard's carefully detailed narrative he demonstrates how with earlier Lutheran influences on the Anglican traditions forgotten until the nineteenth-century, intermarriage with Protestant and Lutheran princes from Denmark and Germany after the deposition of the Catholic King James II brought Lutheran influence into the court. The formation of a Lutheran royal chapel at the Court of St. James by George of Denmark and the chaplain's (Wilhelm Boehm's) influence on the formation of the Society for Promoting Christian Knowledge (SPCK) resulted in Anglican and Lutheran cooperation in sending missionaries to Tranquebar in India, formative for the next essay by J. Jayakiran Sebastian.

Although the Lutherans did not join in the formation of the Church of South India in 1947, the inclusion of bishops served as a model for future agreements. The fact that Lutherans maintained "superintendents" and the Swedish Lutheran Church sustained the historic episcopate made it possible for Lutheran Anglican and Episcopal Lutheran agreements in the late twentieth century in Europe, Canada, and the United States. The Episcopal Church entered full communion with the Evangelical Lutheran Church ("Called to Common Mission," 1999–2000) and the Moravian Church (2009). Similarly Prichard traces parallel agreements in the *Porvoo Agreement* of 1996 between British and Irish Anglicans and Nordic and Baltic Lutherans (1996), the Waterloo Declaration of 2001 by the National Convention of the Evangelical Lutheran Church in Canada and the General Synod of the Anglican Church of Canada (2001), and *Covenanting for Mutual Recognition and Reconciliation* between The Anglican Church of Australia and The Lutheran Church of Australia (2001). In 1997 Martin Luther was added to the minor feasts and celebrations in the Book of Common Prayer. In addition, the International Anglican–Lutheran International Co-ordinating Committee (ALICC) devoted its 2014 meeting to developing "plans for resources through which Lutherans and Anglicans can commemorate together the year 1517."

If Robert Prichard used a variety of histories and documents to construct a narrative in which Lutherans and Anglicans shared a common history alongside each other until the late twentieth century, J. Jayakiran Sebastian, a member of the Church of South India, uses autobiography to show how "this shared history" comes together in the life of a Reformed person in India. Employing a postmodern and postcolonial approach to demonstrate how his Reformed Indian perspective was shaped both positively and negatively by multiple reformation forces, Jayakiran Sebastian argues that context is crucial to understanding the Reformed Reformation. The SPCK's decision to send Lutheran missionaries like Ziegenbalg, the first protestant missionary to Tranqubar in India in the nineteenth century, had implications for his life. He was named Johann Sebastian, by his formerly Hindu father who served as organist in a Scottish Reformed church, St Andrew's, in Bangalore, India. Sebastian describes how the Kirk became increasingly anglicized or "high church" over his life span. Sebastian writes:

> The creation of the Church of South India in 1947 by uniting the South India United Church (Congregational, Presbyterian, and Reformed), the Anglican missions in Southern India, and the Methodist Church of South India signaled for the first time a possible way forward for Anglicans in discussions about church merger. The Church of South India made a discussion between those who were already ordained (who were accepted as validly ordained clergy, whatever their form of ordination) and future ordinations (which were to be by bishops). The CSI is already a modern expression of the Reformation's ecumenical developments . . . The reality is that I'm someone encapsulating within my personal, ecclesiastical and ministerial identity the cosmopolitan hybridity, diversity, promise and potential of the shaking of the foundations set in motion by the Protestant reformation; influenced by the great movements toward the unity of the church in the twentieth century.

If this volume were a four-person relay race Jacob Wood would take the final baton representing the Roman Catholic Church's interaction with the commemorations of the Reformation. In his essay, "The 500th Anniversary of the Reformation: A Catholic Perspective," he has gifted the discussion with a classic essay in intellectual history and Roman Catholic interpretations of Augustine on free choice, the necessity of grace, and the unity of the church for the last five hundred years since the Reformation.

Marking the relevant dates in Roman Catholic history, he narrates how the Reformation began a conversation that challenged the Roman Catholic Church to articulate an Augustinianism, which could account in an integral way for the freedom of the will, the necessity of grace, and the unity of the Church. Debates about free will and grace after the Council of Trent led to a vision of the unity of the Church focused on the pope as the sole absolute monarch on earth, a vision which in turn raised questions about the relationship between unity and freedom. Vatican I failed to define completely the relationship between the pope and the rest of the Church which left open the opportunity for Vatican II to re-envision that relationship as a communion, grounded in the unity of the persons of the Trinity, and freely entered into by grace. This renewed self-understanding opened the Catholic Church to ecumenical dialogue in the decades that followed, and can serve as a basis from which to pursue the goal of complete ecumenical unity today. Woods writes:

> In the years since Vatican II, this renewal of self-understanding has enabled ecumenical progress to proceed at a pace which would have been unthinkable a century ago. One of the most significant fruits of this progress has been the *Joint Declaration on the Doctrine of Justification* made between the Lutheran World Federation and the Pontifical Council for Promoting Christian Unity, in which Catholics recognized the importance of the will in the Lutheran doctrine of justification, and Lutherans recognized the primacy of grace in the Catholic doctrine of justification. That declaration made a bold move towards healing the ecclesial divisions brought about during the Reformation, by returning to one of the principal disagreements that began it in search of reconciliation. Although the *Joint Declaration* did not resolve every disagreement between Catholics and Lutherans on the doctrine of justification,[1] and so full reconciliation.

The Holy Spirit has been at work in the traditions over the last five hundred years to draw the divergent strains of the reformations of the sixteenth century into convergence sometimes in reconciled diversity but always towards unity. We can see that convergence of the streams that flow from these reformations in a single biography, in families, in nations, in movements and institutions, and as a result of ecumenical dialogs and agreements among communions. Thanks be to the God and Father of our Lord Jesus Christ, October 31, 2017, will be commemorated collaboratively

---

1. See "Response of the Catholic Church to the Joint Declaration of the Catholic Church and the Lutheran World Federation on the Doctrine of Justification," http://www.vatican.va/roman_curia/pontifical_councils/chrstuni/documents/rc_pc_chrstuni_doc_01081998_off-answer-catholic_en.html.

and for the sake of the renewal of theology and a common doctor and not over against one another. It is my prayer that October 31 will again return to the occasional minor commemoration that it was in the first centuries after the Reformation so that the major festivals that unite the church like Christmas, Easter, Pentecost, and Trinity Sunday will help us to grow together as one communion of saints in Christ Jesus.

1

Martin Luther and the Lutheran Reformation—October 31, 1517– October 31, 2017

From Augustinian Monk and Doctor of the Church Attempting to Reform Catholic Theology in 1517 to *doctor communis* of the Church in 2017

—Philip D. W. Krey

1517 The "Posting" of the Ninety-Five Theses and Early Commemorations

We may never know whether on October 31, 1517, Martin Luther actually nailed or had a student nail ninety-five theses on the door of the Castle Church or on other Wittenberg church doors. We do know that his colleague and friend Philipp Melanchthon, who arrived in Wittenberg one year later, thought he did. In a vita about Luther in the preface to the second Wittenberg edition of *Luther's Works* (1546) he noted that having been spurred on by Tetzel's preaching and sale of indulgences Luther nailed the Ninety-Five Theses on the door of the Castle Church on October 31, 1517.[1]

---

1. Leppin and Wengert, "Sources for and against the Posting of the Ninety-Five Theses," 373–98. The authors argue that there are arguments on both sides of the issue, and it is impossible to conclude whether he actually nailed the theses to the Chapel door. There was a regulation by the University of Wittenberg that such summons for disputations

Luther's colleague also "held a classroom ceremony for the event out of collegial piety."[2] Martin Luther himself seems to have celebrated the event at home on November 1, 1527, as he reports in a letter to Nikolaus von Amsdorf: "Ten years after the indulgences have been destroyed; in memory of this we both drink and are comforted at this hour."[3] However, there is no mention of his having observed the event in subsequent decades.[4] What we do know is that these Ninety-ive Theses intended as a proposal for reform by "an intentionally Catholic theologian" who knew himself to be a teacher of the church[5] via theological discussion launched a movement when published that eventually divided the church and perhaps the late-medieval and modern worlds. Those divisions are healing after five hundred years and his reform theology is now gradually being accepted as part of the Roman Catholic tradition such that the 500th Anniversary Celebration of the Reformation will observe him more as the common doctor of the church than hero and prophet.

We know that Luther's critique of scholastic theology and his theological concerns with indulgences began earlier than the evening and the day of All Saint's (October 31–November 1) 1517, but this weekend has been etched into the historical imagination over the centuries that this essay will address. Scholars have proposed that Martin Luther's reform can now be understood as the most significant in a series of medieval and late-medieval attempts at reform.[6] In some sense the Roman Catholic Church had become immune to the many attempts at reform from, for example, the Mendicant movements of the thirteenth century that were received by Pope Innocent III to the failed reforms of the Conciliar movement of the fifteenth century that foundered on the reefs of nationalism and a timeless attraction for a strong leader over against a constitutional and balanced papal monarchy. In any event, in the sixteenth century the context left Luther, the Augustinian monk and young professor of theology at the University of

---

were to be posted on all the church doors in Wittenberg. This article includes a comprehensive bibliography of the literature on the sources.

2. WA 1, 230. Piepkorn notes this in "A Lutheran Theologian looks at the Ninety-Five Theses in 1967," 519.

3. Lehmann, *Luthergedächtnis 1817 bis 2017*, 17. See also Wendebourg, "Vergangene Reformationsjubiläen," 262. See the "Letter to Nicolaus von Amsdorf" (WABr 4, 274).

4. See Lehmann, *Luthergedächtnis 1817 bis 2017*, 17.

5. Piepkorn, "A Lutheran Theologian," 523.

6. See for example, Huovinen, "*Doctor communis*: The Ecumenical Significance of Martin Luther's Theology," 137–38.

Wittenberg, with a proposal for reform and a number of secret sympathizers but a hardened church structure that made dialog impossible.[7] He was eventually declared a heretic.[8]

What happened on that critical day?[9] The Augustinian monk and young professor at the University of Wittenberg (age 34), Dr. Martin Luther sent a letter to the Archbishop of Magdeburg–Mainz alerting him of the danger to the proclamation of the Gospel in his territory since the Dominican Friar Johann Tezel was marketing and exaggerating the sale of indulgences. To this letter Luther attached theses arguing theologically against the sale of indulgences.[10] He did not expect the Prince-Bishop to respond to the theses, as the disputation was the right and duty of the university.[11] Thus Luther was working on this issue for some time. The Wittenberg faculty including Andreas Karlstadt was preparing for theological debate.[12] Luther had been researching the ecclesiastical, theological, and legal grounds for indulgences earlier in 1517 and was distressed by the great collection of relics that Prince Frederick had stored at the Castle Church—the list of which would be read publicly on All Saints Day, November 1. Historians agree that whether or not the Theses were posted, the events of the days lose none of their historical importance.[13] To some extent Luther was surprised by the broad reception that the Theses received. That the subsequent sermon "On Indulgences and Grace" (Feb. 2, 1518) in German enjoyed at least twenty editions surprised Luther.[14] What was and remains decisive is the

---

7. Piepkorn, "A Lutheran Theologian," 523: "In all these documents Luther writes as an intentionally Catholic theologian who could rightly point out that he had his ordinary's imprimatur—not hastily given either—both for the "Sermon von dem Ablass und Gnade" and for the "Resolutiones disputationum de indulgentiarum virtute" (and with the latter, for the Ninety-Five Theses that the latter incorporated."

8. See the bibliography in Kaufmann, *A Short Life of Martin Luther*.

9. See Heinrich Bornkamm, "Thesen und Thesenanschlag Luthers, 1–7."

10. Lehmann, *Luthergedächtnis*, 17.

11. Bornkamm, *Thesen*, 4.

12. See Manns and Pelikan, *Martin Luther*, 89–94.

13. Leppin and Wengert, "Sources for and against the Posting of the Ninety-Five Theses," 373. See also note 5. For new translations of and introductions to three of the most important documents from 1517–1518, see "The 95 Theses," "The 31 October 1517 Letter to Archbishop Albrecht," and "The Sermon on Indulgences and Grace," 1–65.

14. Leppin and Wengert cite Luther from the "Sermon on Indulgences and Grace" (WA 1:528, 38–529, 2): "They [the Theses] were published only among our own and for our own. Then, once they were published—what seems to me unbelievable—they became known to everyone. For they were simply [theses for] disputation, not doctrine

Reformation's proposal to the church catholic, a proclamation of the gospel that continues to challenge and influence Lutheran, Reformed, and Roman Catholic Christians to this day.[15]

What we also know is that as the Reformation movement developed the nailing of the Theses was not the focus of commemorations but the life events of Martin Luther himself—his birth and death dates—and the anniversaries of key Reformation events—the establishment of Lutheranism in different territories, the Diet of Augsburg, or the *Book of Concord*. To some extent the date and event itself was lost to history for a century and the message was overshadowed by the larger than life figure of Luther, himself and the movement that the content of the theses set in motion.

Given the context of the church and personalities involved, the movement that was launched, in particular, by the mailing of the Theses and later explanations unleashed forces that were irreversible and hurtled towards schism and not for the Wittenberg faculty's hoped for theological discussion. Tetzel felt compelled to respond and Eck took it upon himself to challenge Luther.[16] Given that Luther himself was soon considered a "prophet teacher and hero" by his followers the anniversaries of his birth and death took on importance.[17] Already at his death in 1546 in his funeral oration Johannes Bugenhagen compared him to the angel with the eternal gospel from Revelation 14:6–7.[18] Like St Francis of Assisi, who was similarly compared to this angel of the apocalypse, Luther was given eschatological and mythological significance by his followers making his anniversary dates overshadow October 31.

1617 The Centennial

Not until 1617 as the schism in the Western church seemed to be permanent and just before the Thirty-Years war was there a specific observance of October 31, nor did the events of that year establish a custom of observing October 31 with worship services or special celebrations. Before then, no particular day or moment had been identified as the beginning of the Reformation. Each territory or city usually celebrated the day when it

---

or dogma, and, as is customary, more obscure and enigmatic," 386.
15. Leppin and Wengert, "Sources for and against the Posting," 390.
16. Manns and Pelikan, *Martin Luther*, 94.
17. Kolb, *Martin Luther as Prophet, Teacher, Hero*.
18. Ibid., 35.

became officially Lutheran and the 25th of June, the Day that the Augsburg Confession was presented in 1530 by Chancellor Christian Beyer to the assembled estates of the Holy Roman Empire of the German Nation was also observed through the sixteenth century. Because Luther was also celebrated as a "prophet, teacher, and hero"[19] his birthday (November 10) or baptismal date (November 11—St. Martin's Day) as also his death date February 18 were often celebrated.[20] The 31st of October was hardly observed at the beginning of the Reformation until 1617 when leading Protestants in Saxony realized that it was now a hundred years since the moment when, on 31 October 1517, Luther had first publicly challenged the authority of the Pope—by, so it is said, posting his Ninety- Five Theses on to the door of the Castle Church at Wittenberg in Saxony.

In January of 1617, the pope began the year with a prayer calling for a reunification of Christendom and for the eradication of heretics. In part in response to the pope's tacit war against them, Lutherans responded with the first Reformation celebration, October 31, 1617. On April 22 the Faculty of the University of Wittenberg asked the Elector of Saxony to declare October 31, 1617, as the first Lutheran Jubilee.[21] The Jubilee was established for worship services for October 31–November 2. Hartmut Lehman has summarized the content of about one hundred printed sermons from this jubilee.[22] Of these he examined the ones preached on the 31st of October. Some preachers compared Luther to the Angel of the Apocalypse of Revelation 14:6 as he proclaimed the eternal gospel to the whole earth.[23] Later this passage would become an assigned lesson to be read at the festival of the Reformation. For all the preachers Luther restored the authority of

19. Ibid.

20. For example in Braunschweig on the first Sunday after September 1 or in Hamburg and Lübeck, Trinity Sunday, the Sunday after Pentecost. Lehmann, *Luthergedächtnis*, 18–19.

21. In the Roman Catholic Church, a jubilee year was ordinarily celebrated every twenty-five years in which a plenary indulgence was granted after penance. A jubilee had its origins in the Jewish biblical custom of freeing slaves, returning lands with liens to their owners, and leaving fields untilled every fifty years. See also Wendebourg, "Vergangene Reformationsjubiläen," 263.

22 Lehmann, *Luthergedächtnis*, 19–21. See also Kolb, *Martin Luther as Prophet, Teacher, Hero*, 126–33.

23 Lehmann also notes that in these sermons he is compared to Noah, Moses as the leader of the Reformation, and Elijah who was promised at the last days, 20. Wendebourg, "*Vergangene Reformationsjubiläen*," 267. describes this as an eschatological message that is lost in subsequent observances especially with the development of Pietism.

Scripture, translated the Word of God into German making it accessible to the laity, corrected the doctrines of justification and the sacraments, and clarified the vocations of secular rulers as well as the institution of the family and marriage. Despite all of this a tradition of celebrating October 31st did not come out of this Jubilee.

There was, however, a broad sheet printed in Leipzig in 1617. Leipzig was the center of the European printing trade at the time.[24] It dramatically depicted a prophetic dream that Duke Frederick the Wise supposedly had the night before October 31, 1517.[25] The editor of the broadsheet claimed that the story of Frederick's dream had been narrated by Frederick's chaplain, Georg Spalatin.[26] When the broadsheet was made, European Protestants were facing an uncertain and dangerous future. Given that the Pope was effectively summoning the Catholic Church to arms against the Reformation, it was clear to everybody that a terrible religious war was about to break out and the broadsheet and the celebration were designed to encourage the Lutherans. Hans Herbele, a Lutheran cobbler, wrote in his diary about the celebration in 1617, "The anniversary festival was the beginning of the war, for one can read frequently in the Catholic records how the sight of this celebration stuck painfully in their eyes."[27] The Thirty-Years war broke out the following year.

According to notes prepared for the exhibit of the print by the curator of the British Museum, the Protestants tried to find a way of rallying their supporters for the fight but, unlike the Catholic Church, they had no central authority to issue directions to the faithful. Protestants had to find other ways of insisting that the Reformation had, in fact, been part of God's plan for the world. That individuals had no need of priests to gain access to God's mercy, that the Roman church was corrupt, and that Luther's Reformation was essential to the salvation of every living soul. Above all, they needed a view of their past that would give all Protestants strength to face

---

24. From the curator's note of the copy in the British Museum; "The print was produced in 1617 in Leipzig, Saxony, one of the major centers of seventeenth-century printing in Europe. It shows a dream of Luther's protector, Frederick the Wise, The Elector of Saxony, in which he foresees Luther's central role in the re-shaping of Christendom. It is an early example of the centenary celebration." This note and the following detailed discussion is drawn from a podcast from the BBC and the British Museum in the series, "A History of the World in 100 Objects," #85, December 23, 2011.

25. Kolb, *Martin Luther as Prophet, Teacher, Hero*, 128–29.

26. Stephens, *Performing the Reformation*, 20.

27. Lund, *Documents from the History of Lutheranism, 1517–1750*, 174.

the terrifying future. With a masterly sense of media management, they launched the first centenary celebration in the modern sense of the word. All the now familiar razzmatazz was there . . . ceremonies and processions, souvenirs, medals, paintings, printed sermons, and this broadsheet—a woodblock print that illustrates the critical day that Protestants now saw as the beginning of the first step on their radical religious journey.[28]

> It's a crowded composition, but the key message is quite clear. In a dream, God is revealing to the Elector of Saxony the historic role of Martin Luther. We see the Elector asleep. Below him, Luther reads the Bible in a great shaft of light coming down from Heaven, where the Trinity is blessing him. As Luther looks up, light and blessings pour down onto the page in front of him. Scripture is literally the revealed word of God, and to read scripture is to encounter God, and this is not happening inside a church. You couldn't have a simpler statement that, for Protestants, Bible reading is the foundation of faith. A foundation which, thanks to the new technology of printing, was now available to all believers, in their own home.
>
> At the front of the print is Luther writing on the church door, with the world's biggest quill pen, the words "vom ablas," "about indulgence"—the title of his virulent attack on the Catholic sale of indulgences, the system by which, in return for cash, you spent less time in purgatory . . . Luther's quill is at least twice the size of himself, and it stretches half way across the print, to a walled city—helpfully labelled Rome—and straight through the head of a lion labelled Pope Leo X, who squats on top of the city. And as if that weren't enough, the quill then knocks the papal crown off the head of the Pope, shown in human form. Never was a pen mightier than this one. The message is coarse but clear. Luther, inspired by reading the scriptures, has destroyed papal authority by the power of his pen.[29]

Woodblocks like this are the first mass media, with print-runs of up to tens of thousands, so that each single copy cost just a few 'pfennigs', the price of a pair of sausages or a couple of pints of ale. Satirical prints like this one would be pinned up in inns and market places, and then widely discussed. When 1717 came around, and new broadsheets were produced to celebrate the bicentenary of Luther nailing his Theses to the church door, the whole

---

28. This broadsheet is also discussed by Kolb, 126–29.
29. "A History of the World in 100 Objects," #85

7

continent was well on the way to another revolution, just as profound as the Reformation and, in many ways, a consequence of the Enlightenment.[30]

1717 The Bicentennial

In 1717 or the bicentennial of October 31, 1517 the Reformation was still a Lutheran celebration, but Lutherans were not fighting for their survival and the annual festival services were commemorated more regularly. In addition, October 31 fell on a Sunday that year. In the introduction to the volume, *Interpreters of Luther*, Jeroslav Pelikan claims for Luther what the Polish Literary critic, Jan Kott, had said of Shakespeare that he "is like the world or like life itself. Every epoch finds in him what it itself is seeking and what it itself wants to imitate."[31] By this celebration Luther had already been claimed by the orthodox Lutherans in the sixteenth and seventeenth centuries as well as the pietists and the rationalists of the seventeenth and eighteenth centuries. Scott Landry argues that if the centennial of Reformation was celebrated as a confessional and orthodox Lutheran event, the bicentennial may have been dominated more by those influenced by Pietism, a renewal movement founded by Philipp Jacob Spener (1635-1705) and continued by August Herman Francke (1663-1727) that responded to rationalism and the devastation of the Thirty-Years War.[32]

The bicentennial was an event in which for the first time coins and medals were minted for the celebration as the nailing of the theses begins to take on more heroic and legendary power. Barry Stephen argues that it is noteworthy that there are not visual depictions of Luther nailing the Ninety-Five Theses on the chapel door until the broadsheet of 1617 that depicts Frederick the Wise's dream sequence. The Ninety-Five Theses in bronze on the chapel doors only occurred in 1858 and the original doors have been lost. Nevertheless, of the 180 coins and medals minted for the celebrations of 1717 only three use as their theme, Luther nailing the theses on the door. Stephen notes, "The image of a defiant, rebellious hammering of the theses to the door of the castle church, however, is the stuff of legend, cultivated over the years through visual culture, stories, sermon, biographies, and on

---

30. Ibid.
31. Cited in Pelikan, *Interpreters of Luther*, 6.
32. Landry, *Ecumenism, Memory, and German Nationalism 1817-1917*, 7.

stage and screen." This he notes develops over the later centuries especially in the nineteenth and twentieth centuries.[33]

Wilhelm Dilthey noted that "the true significance of Luther and his Reformation cannot be fully appreciated merely on the basis of works of dogmatics. Its documents are the writings of Luther, the church chorale, the sacred music of Bach and Handel, and the structure of community life in the church."[34] Music so central to Luther and the Reformation tradition was also a way of commemorating the event and the Feast of the Reformation was observed in Leipzig on October 31, 1717. In electoral Saxony the regular observance of October 31 was established in 1667, on the 150th anniversary of Luther's posting of the Ninety-Five Theses. As noted earlier, the Reformation anniversary was never considered fully equal to the principal festivals of the church year, despite its increasing significance in the eighteenth century.[35] This is reflected in Bach's hymn book, "Das Neu Leipziger Gesangbuch" of 1682, where there is no separate listing of hymns to be sung for the Festival of the Reformation.[36] Meanwhile the recognized Reformation chorales are found in the appropriate thematic sections of Trinity Time such as "Psalm Hymns" ("Ein feste Burg ist unser Gott," No. 255) and "Christian Life and Conduct" ("Nun danket alle Gott," No. 238). These were assigned for *Reformation Vespers*.[37]

33. Stephens, *Performing the Reformation*, 20.
34. Cited in Pelikan, *Bach Among the Theologians*, 17.
35. Stiller, *JSB and Liturgical Life in Leipzig*, 85.
36. In contrast the early Common Service hymnals in the United States have a section for the Festival of The Reformation even if there are only three hymns listed. *The Common Service Book* and Hymnal of the Lutheran Church issued in October 1917 for the quadricentennial year that follows Henry Melchior Muhlenberg's hymnal of 1786, however, though it lists October 31 as the Festival of the Reformation, does not have a section devoted to the Reformation. It notes that, "In the compilation of the *Hymnal* the Committee has sought to include the largest possible number of the classical hymns of the Church of all lands and times, particularly those which were produced in the age and by the spirit of the Protestant Reformation." "Preface to the Common Service Book, 1917 of the Lutheran Church," 309.
37 Reformation Festive Vespers were held in Leipzig on the eve of the festival. The music may have included the organ Prelude, "Ein feste Burg ist unser Gott," BWV 720; Psalm 46 setting, "Ein feste Burg ist unser Gott" (NLGB No. 255); German Magnificat, "Meine Seele erhebt den Herrn" (NLGB No. 153); Cantata BWV 80; Versicles; Nunc dimittis, Canticum Simeonis (NLGB No. 55); Collects; Benediction; Recessional Hymn, "Nun danket alle Gott" (NLGB No. 238); and organ chorale postlude, "Nun danket alle Gott," BWV 657. (See Recording information: Frederick Grimes & Holy Trinity Bach Choir, http://www.bach-cantatas.com/Performers/Grimes-F.htm).

The catalogs of works of Johann Sebastian Bach, The fifth evangelist, whose music and lyrics demonstrate a brilliant combination of traditional catholic affective piety and Lutheran proclamation,[38] list only two cantatas—BWV 80, "Ein feste Burg ist unser Gott," and BWV 79, "Gott der Herr ist Sonn und Schild"—as main sacred service musical sermons Sebastian composed for and presented at an annual Reformation Festival. Bach, who was steeped in Luther's theology and hymnody proclaimed the message of Luther's Reformation in music. "Gott der Herr ist Sonn und Schild," a joyous, dancing quarter-hour cantata, was first performed October 31, 1725 and dedicated to the Feast of the Reformation. The iconic half-hour chorale cantata, BWV 80, that evolved for two decades in at least four versions—the second of which is lost but was specifically adapted for the Reformation Festival, October 31, 1728—was first composed in Weimar in 1715 for the third Sunday in Lent but since cantatas were not sung in Lent it was performed in 1724 at the Lutherfest in Leipzig. and dedicated to the Feast of the Reformation.[39] These cantatas and their dedications indicate that the Festival of the Reformation was being observed at least in Weimar and Leipzig on a regular, if not, annual basis.[40] Although still limited to the world of Lutheranism, the observance of October 31 is captured by the imagination of artists and musicians.

1817 The Tercentennial

According to Dorothea Wendebourg, the three-hundredth anniversary, in 1817 was the game changer.[41] Stan Landry argues that the commemora-

---

38. See Wilkens, "Lutheran Pietism and Catholic Piety," 79–92.

39. See Pelikan, *Bach Among the Theologians*, 16. See also, Hoffman, Bach Cantatas & Other Vocal Works; BCW, http://www.bach-cantatas.com/Performers/Grimes-F.htm#C1] Possible *Reformation Cantatas*. See also Dürr, *The Cantatas of J. S. Bach*.

40. "It appears that an altered-text version of Cantata BWV 63 by Gottfried Kirchoff (1685–1746), Halle organist, was presented during the bicentennial Jubilee Festival of the Reformation in Halle's Liebfrauen Kirche, October 31, 1717. Its text is found in a printed collection of festival sermons and commentaries, compiled in 1718 by Johann Michael Heineccius (1674–1722), church pastor, to whom the text is attributed. Heineccius officiated at Bach's probe on Dec. 13, 1713, to succeed Friedrich Wilhem Zachow, Handel's teacher. At that time it is believed that Bach could have presented a version of Cantata 63 that omitted the recitatives that later were revised for the Reformation. Source," William Hoffman, "Cantata 63, BCW Discussion 3, http://www.bach-cantatas.com/BWV63-D3.htm, (February 9, 2009.).

41. Wendebourg, "Vergangene Reformationsjubiläen," 269. See also Thomas Albert

tion expanded beyond Lutherans and included Roman Catholics and some Jews.[42] Noll summarizes: "In 1806, Napoleon had dissolved the Holy Roman Empire and the influence of the American and French revolutions was in ascendance. During the preceding century, the congeries of movements and ideas we call the Enlightenment had effected a steady mutation in how Europeans remembered the Reformation. For philosophers and enlightened Protestants alike, the Reformation had become less an act of religious recovery than a catalyst toward the path of bourgeois liberties and civilizational progress. The German Kaiser William Frederick III had initiated the union of the Lutheran and Reformed churches in the German lands and written his own liturgy for common worship. The unification was initiated on the Tercentennial of the Reformation to establish a shared religious basis for the unification of Germany. Friedrich Schleiermacher, The dean of the theology faculty of the University of Berlin, celebrated this union and interpreted the Reformation in the light of the progress of Protestantism towards a modern critical approach to religion."[43] Now, Roman Catholicism was less a false church (Though Schleiermacher was most critical of its dogmas and cultic practices) than a historical impediment to progress, a cauldron of ignorance and superstition that vexed and oppressed the human spirit. The early stirrings of nationalism, not least in the German lands, were also ominously apparent both before and during the 1817 commemorations. Themes of liberty and progress in particular peppered the homilies and orations from 1817.[44]

On October 18, 1817, a group of German University students with liberal and nationalist tendencies, many of whom were veterans of the wars of liberation, assembled at the Wartburg Castle in Eisenach united under the mantra of "Honor, Freedom, and Fatherland." The students agitated for a reform of German colleges, demanded the liberal constitution that King Frederick Wilhelm had promised, and encouraged the unification of the German states. During the gathering the students celebrated Luther as a German citizen and patriot who had embodied the liberal characteristics of reason, virtue, and freedom. The celebrants sang the Lutheran hymn,

---

Howell and Mark Noll, "The Reformation at Five Hundred," *First Things* (Nov. 2014) 45–48.

42. Landry, *Ecumenism, Memory, and German Nationalism 1817–1917*, 3.

43. There was however a strong reaction from some Lutherans, who called themselves "Alt or "Old" Lutherans" and they eventually wanted to form their own church. This was especially true in Silesia.

44. Howell and Noll, "The Reformation at Five Hundred," 45.

"A Mighty Fortress," which Heinrich Heine would later call the German Marseillaise, along with other patriotic songs.[45] The year 1817 and its celebrations proved to be a defining moment for German nationalism leading to the unification of the German Empire in 1871.[46]

If in 1518 Luther's sermon on Indulgences and grace enjoyed at least twenty editions, in 1817 an image of the Ninety-Five Theses being posted went "viral."[47] In addition to Luther depicted in a domesticated family setting playing music with his children around him, the scenes depict a student proxy posting the theses while Luther and others engage in theological discussion alongside the image of the reformer burning the bull of excommunication and his defense before Emperor Charles V at Worms in 1521. Georg Paul Buckner of Nuremberg was the first to depict Luther prominently posting the theses for the 300th anniversary of October 31, 1517, as part of a sixteen-scene life of Luther.[48] "This image with that of his burning the bull and his defense at Worms formed a kind of mental triptych for the post-Enlightenment liberal spirit of the times: Luther first shows that reason cannot always trust tradition and authority."[49]

The celebration of 1817 also produced a host of Luther and Reformation commemorations because this was also the era of historicism:[50] The 300th anniversary of the Augsburg Confession in 1830, the 300th anniversary of Luther's death in 1846, the 200th anniversary of the Peace of Westphalia in 1848, the 300th anniversary if the Peace of Augsburg in 1855, and the 350th anniversary of Luther's challenge to indulgences in 1867. The earlier celebration of 1617 and 1717 rehearsed the ideas and theologies of 1517, but the commemoration of 1817 represents the developing liberalism, nationalism, especially German nationalism, and historicism that defined that part of the nineteenth century.[51] According to Howell and Noll, the "Reformation had become less an act of religious recovery than a catalyst toward the path of bourgeois liberties and civilizational progress."[52] Heinrich Böhmer, who wrote *Luther in the Light of Recent Research* for the

45. Landry, *Ecumenism, Memory*, 3.
46. Ibid., 4.
47. Howell and Noll, *The Reformation at Five Hundred*, 45.
48. Lehmann, *Luthergedächtnis 1817 bis 2017*, 25.
49. Howard, "Remembering the Reformation, 1817 and 1883," 129.
50. Howell and Noll, 46.
51. Howard, *Remembering the Reformation*, 125.
52. Howell and Noll, *The Reformation at Five Hundred*, 45.

New York Reformation Quadicentenary Committee (1917) similarly, summarizes the spirit of this commemoration.[53] Thomas A. Howard concludes that the jubilee of 1817 and 1883 were not "simply conduits or transmitters of the old but definers and harbingers of the new, in this sense, we might view these jubilees, not unlike the sixteenth-century Reformation itself: a series of acts motivated by the desire of retrieval and restoration, that in the final analysis, left a legacy of profound change, disruption, and innovation in human history."[54] In his book *Luther in the Light of Recent Research*, Böhmer captures the spirit of this jubilee of 1817 by citing a hymn written for the occasion:

> List, ye me and be advised,
> No more in shackles the spirit lies.
>> Remember Luther, the faithful one,
>> Who hath this freedom for you won,
> Guard well the light, the light of truth,
> Guard well the fire, profane it not.[55]

1917 The Quadricentennial

The Quadricenntenial served as a proleptic event to mark the end of optimism of the liberalism and the faith in progress of the nineteenth-century celebrations. Karl Barth's *Commentary on Romans* in 1918 challenged the liberal confidence in the progress of modernity with a radical "No" to human achievement. Although Martin Luther was recognized in Germany as a national hero, it was losing the First World War with the entrance of the United States into war that had pitted proud nationalistic Christian nations against each other. In the United States great plans were set forth to market the contributions of Lutherans, who were then the third largest denomination among Protestants in the United States to the culture and economy even though there were few Lutherans in public office at the time. Mark Grandquist writes, "There was much talk about rededication, confessional loyalty, and bold witness among all the branches of Lutherans including the Missouri Synod with an eschatological expectation that the papacy would soon end. The pan Lutheran celebration was to represent "The coming of

---

53. Böhmer, *Luther in the Light of Recent Research*, 28.
54. Howard, *Remembering the Reformation*, 125.
55. Böhmer, *Luther in the Light of Recent Research*, 12.

age of American Lutheranism."[56] The planning was marred for this immigrant church by the declaration of war against Germany on Good Friday, April 8, 1917, even though most celebrations did occur albeit scaled back and focused on human sinfulness and the need for Luther's teaching.[57] Traditions of German origin were suddenly less popular and marketable.

In 1883 Lutherans who wished to lift up the influence of Luther in the United States succeeded in mounting monumental statues of Luther in Baltimore and Washington, DC, the nation's capital. In 1917, however, when with funds raised by Sunday School children an imposing monument of Henry Melchior Muhlenberg, the patriarch of American Lutheranism, was presented for the Quadricentennial to the City of Philadelphia to be set in Fairmount Park, it was refused by the city due to anti-German sentiment. It was moved to the entrance of the new location of the Lutheran Theological Seminary in Mt. Airy, Philadelphia.[58]

There were already earlier signs that the American Lutheranism hoped for by Samuel Simon Schmucker, President of the Lutheran Theological Seminary at Gettysburg, who like Philip Schaff had worked in the "Evangelical Alliance" for a union of the major protestant denominations would run into resistance. American Lutheranism like Lutheranism in the earlier commemorations had been in an identity crisis as opponents to this trend, like Charles Porterfield Krauth (1823–1883) of the Lutheran Theological Seminary at Philadelphia, insisted upon Lutheran confessional identity over against an American Protestantism.[59] It is ironic that the visions of Schmucker and Krauth were realized in the late twentieth century as these Protestant denominations entered full communion while respecting one another's confessional identities.

Philip Schaff had planned for the 400th anniversary of Luther's birth in 1883 to be a celebration of American Protestantism. E. Theodore Bachman writes:

> It was Schaff who spearheaded the move to make the 1883 meeting of the Alliance's American branch and observance of the 400th anniversary of Luther's birth. This was in the context of celebrations,

---

56. Granquist, *A New History*, 224.

57. Nelson, *The Lutherans in North America*, 394.

58. During the observances of the 150th anniversary of the seminary in Philadelphia in 2014 Mayor Michael Nutter formerly rescinded the city's rejection of the statue.

59. The first two anniversary commemorations also focused on Lutheranism's confessional identity and theological contributions.

as he put it, "throughout Protestant Christendom." The Alliance issued invitations to the Protestant churches in the United States to celebrate Luther's birthday by sermons on the Reformation. The sermons and addresses in the church periodicals the autumn of 1883 are but a few of the many which set forth Luther's "merits as a man and a German, as husband and father, as a preacher, catechist, and hymnist, as a Bible translator, and expositor, as a reformer and founder of a church, as a champion of the sacred right of conscience, an originator of a mighty movement of religious and civil liberty which spread over Europe and across the Atlantic to the shores of the Pacific.[60]

Antipapal sentiment especially after Vatican 1 (1869–1870) and American nativism in response to Roman Catholic immigration that was shared by most Lutherans who wished to be Americanized at the time was shared by other traditions. Lutherans were not alone in recognizing October 31, 1917. The observance of the General Assembly of the Presbyterian Church in the United States of America in Dallas Texas in May of that year is emblematic of protestant views. In preparation for the celebration, the General Assembly of 1916, in session in Atlantic City, took action:

> To provide for the celebration of the four hundredth anniversary of the Protestant Reformation which began with the posting of the Ninety-five Theses on the church door in Wittenberg by Martin Luther, October 31, 1517: Whereas, The four hundredth anniversary of the Protestant Reformation occurs in 1917; and Whereas, The Churches constituting the Council of the Reformed Churches holding the Presbyterian System represent historically one great branch of the Christian Church of the Reformation. Therefore, be it resolved, that the Council recommends to the several supreme judicatories the holding of suitable anniversary services for the purpose of emphasizing the great principles of the Reformation of the sixteenth century[61]

The Quadricentennial captured what a focus Lutheran and in general Protestant identity had brought to these commemorations. The keynoter at the Assembly, Dr. David S, Schaff, Philip's son, delivered a panegyric for

60. Schaff, *History of the Christian Church*, 730. Cited in Bachman, "Walther, Schaff, and Krauth on Luther," 190–91.

61 "Be it Resolved, That, in connection with whatever celebration of the Luther Anniversary may be arranged for 1917 all Presbyterian churches be called upon to commemorate the nailing of the Theses on the door of the Wittenberg Church . . ." "Minutes," 1916, 309.

Luther and the Reformation. He would highlight in high-sounding rhetoric the heroic accomplishments of Luther and the Reformation that would change over the century as a result of ecumenical dialog and work in what H Lehmann calls the "demythologization" of the Luther in the 20th century.[62]

THE ADDEESS BEFORE THE GENERAL ASSEMBLY
THE ORIGIN AND PURPOSE OF THE
PROTESTANT REFORMATION
Mr. Moderator, Members of the Assembly,
Ladies, and Gentlemen:

The Protestant Reformation, the four hundredth anniversary of which we are now commemorating, is the most memorable event since the days of the apostles. It marked the close of the Middle Ages and ushered in these modern centuries. It was a protest against the ecclesiastical system built up by the practice of able pontiffs and justified by the acute reasoning of the Schoolmen. It was more than a protest: It was a reproclamation of the gospel. It announced emancipation from the papal monarchy. It brought release from bondage to the priesthood, which claimed as a monopoly the function of mediating between the soul and God. It gave the Scriptures to the common man. It republished salvation by free grace. It asserted for all alike the right to go at once for pardon and life to the chief Bishop and Shepherd of our souls. It proclaimed the sovereignty of the individual man. Setting aside the monastic ideal, it taught once more the true use of the world and the dignity of all legitimate human occupations; it taught that every creature of God is good, and nothing to be despised, if it be received with thanksgiving.

The impulse which gave the Reformation birth was wholly religious. Social and economic unrest prevailed in the sixteenth century as in the twentieth. Social and economic changes were engaging the dreams and speculation of the age—not all Utopian. Social and economic betterments followed the preaching of the Reformers. But, in the first instance, and all through, the Reformers had it as their controlling aim to reannounce the plain way whereby a man may be just with God . . .

---

62 The address was delivered before the General Assembly, Saturday, May 19. Rev. Wallace Eadcliffe, D.D., LL.D., pastor of the New York Avenue Presbyterian Church, Washington, DC, and a former Moderator of the Assembly, presided. In introducing the speaker, Dr. Eadcliffe spoke of the importance of the Reformation and the distinction of the speaker's father, Dr. Philip Schaff, as a Church historian.

Schaff continued to relate how the Reformation swept the world from Wittenberg and the rest of Europe to the Americas and after lamenting the disunity among Protestants narrated Luther's life and the career of the reformer in heroic terms.

If as is noted in this speech, Luther the person and the events surrounding his life were observed together the quadricentennial also coincided with Karl Holl's (1866–1926) precipitation of the Luther Renaissance of the twentieth century with his seminal essays refocusing Luther scholarship on Luther's understanding of justification, the political ramifications of his theology, his understanding of the church, and "What did Luther Understand by Religion?" (A festival lecture delivered at the University of Berlin on October 31, 1917). Although some of Holl's theses have been found to be limited, he not only taught major Luther scholars of the twentieth century but also provided a rigor in scholarship that moved past "ideological prejudices" that had influenced former centuries. The publication of the critical edition of Luther's Works beginning in 1883 also helped his scholarship and that of the Luther renaissance to follow.[63] As Luther was read as a whole he was also read by Roman Catholic scholars who began especially after Vatican II to see him within the catholic tradition even if radically so. In the twentieth century Luther's limitations were also recognized as he was demythologized especially in his writings against the peasants and his anti-Semitic writings given the horrors of the holocaust in Hitler's Germany. Eric Gritsch, for example concludes:

> Although Luther was decisively influenced by Paul in his "theology of the cross" anchored in the doctrine of "justification by grace through faith rather than the works of the law," he ignored, indeed rejected Paul's "eschatological reservation" for Jewish Christian unity (Rom 11:25–32). Luther succumbed to speculations about the fate of the Jews as victims of divine wrath for their refusal to convert: God canceled the old covenant with Abraham, prefiguring salvation in Christ, because the Jews transformed it into a Talmudic Judaism of self-righteousness based on laws without a Messiah. These speculations violated Luther's own theological judgment against any claims to know the will of the "hidden God" (*deus absconditus*) and be satisfied with the knowledge about the "revealed God" (*deus revelatus*)—as he argued against Erasmus in 1525 [in the *Bondage of the Will*]. The core of his theology anchored in "the justification of the ungodly" through faith in Christ,

---

63. Lohse, *Martin Luther*, 223–25.

agreed with Paul that God "will justify the circumcised on the ground of faith and the uncircumcised through the same faith" (Rom 3:10). Such "good news," the gospel, is part of a dialectic with the "law." It leads to repentance, preceded by spiritual anxiety and suffering (*Anfechtung*); the gospel leads to salvation fully realized after Christ's second coming. But Luther was sliding into a theological speculation about the Jews against his better judgment grounded in Paul, namely, that faith in Christ can never "justify" the divine punishment of the Jews. They, together with the Christian Gentiles, share the interim leading to a full union when Christ will come again.[64]

The Luther Renaissance and the study of Luther's writings in his context also revealed his indebtedness to the tradition which he both criticized and appropriated. There was an explosion of Luther biographies in the twentieth century.[65] Scholars like Heiko Oberman also showed through intense research of late-medieval theology that Luther both continues and broke with theological debates that prevailed in the schools before him.[66] Like other great reformers before him Augustine and Aquinas through intense scholarship, life as a monk and priest and professor, prayer, and reading—no devouring texts—he plumbed them and came out having turned them upside down and renewed. Scholars of the twentieth century began to recognize the value and contribution of the tradition and Luther's appreciation for it so that he needed not always represent the liberal ideals of newness and human progress but no matter how radical—retrieval and preservation of the message of Paul and to some extent a revision of Augustine.[67]

This same century which became the ecumenical century launched the mergers of Lutheran denominations in the United States and around the world and was also the century in which the Lutheran World Federation

---

64. Gritsch, *Martin Luther's Anti-Semistism*, 140–41.

65. See, for example, Hendrix, "American Luther Research in the Twentieth Century," 1–23.

66 See for example, Oberman, *Forerunners of the Reformation*; and Oberman, *The Dawn of the Reformation*.

67. See, for example, Pelikan, *Obedient Rebels*. In addition, the common return to a revitalization of tradition can be seen especially in the Liturgical Renewal Movement in the twentieth century. It has affected the shape and renewal of the liturgy and celebrated the assembly in the Pauline image of the "mystical body of Christ" that has revitalized the Roman Catholic, Lutheran, and other mainstream liturgies together. Pecklers and Spinks, "The Liturgical Movement," 283–89.

was formed (1947).⁶⁸ There was a growing sense that the Lutheran movement had become an ecumenical movement in the church catholic and by the power of the Holy Spirit the rifts of sixteenth century could be healed. After fifty years of ecumenical dialog an historic agreement was reached on October 31, 1999, when representatives of The Lutheran World Federation representing 72 million Lutherans worldwide and the Vatican signed *The Joint Declaration on Justification* in Augsburg, Germany declaring that the key issue in Paul's Letter to the Romans and the Reformation of the sixteenth century was no longer church dividing.

Already in the Fifth Assembly of the Lutheran World Federation (1970) Cardinal Jan Willebrands applied the classic Roman Catholic title of *doctor communis* (a common teacher) to Martin Luther and referred to Luther's teaching that "justification by grace through faith" is the doctrine upon which the church stands or falls."⁶⁹ This title is one of the honorifics of St Thomas Aquinas meaning that according to Cardinal Willebrands, St. Thomas, the Middle ages, and the Reformation belong together. Luther represented and continued a common tradition. This tradition is also a resource for the future for Roman Catholics and Protestants alike the *Joint Declaration on Justification* (1988) confirmed.⁷⁰

The 500th Anniversary of Luther's birth in 1983⁷¹ also promoted interest in Luther as the Father of the German language and culture in

---

68. Schjorring et al., *From Federation to Communion*.

69. See Huovinen, "*Doctor communis?*," 137.

70 "[T]he *Joint Declaration,* officially signed by representatives of the Catholic Church and the Lutheran World Federation on October 31, 1999, in Augsburg Germany, states that Lutherans and Catholics have achieved a consensus in basic truths of the doctrine of justification (JD 40). It states that the teaching of the Lutheran churches and of the Roman Catholic Church found therein does not fall under the condemnations formulated in the sixteenth century by the Council of Trent and the Lutheran Confessions towards the other's view of the doctrine (cf. JD 41). When Edward Idris Cardinal Cassidy, President of the Pontifical Council for Promoting Christian Unity, made public the Catholic Church's formal approval of the JD on June 25, 1998, he stated the achievement that the JD represents in relation to sixteenth-century divisions in this way: 'the consensus reached on the doctrine of justification despite its limitations virtually resolves a long disputed question at the close of the twentieth century...'" Radano, *Lutheran and Catholic Reconciliation on Justification*, xxi–xxii. See also the official documents he lists in the notes on p. xxii.

71. The United States Postal Service issued a commemorative 20 cent stamp for the year. It was designed by Bradbury Thompson, a design coordinator for the Postal Service's Citizens's Advisory Committee, and was based on a 1533 portrait by Lucas Cranach the Elder (1472–1553). The stamp was officially issued on Thursday, November 10 in

Western Germany and in the East as Germany was still divided Luther was celebrated along with Karl Marx, whose centennial occurred in the same year, as a revolutionary and an advocate for the socialism. Posters of Marx and Luther hung side by side in exhibits across the nation.[72] For both countries religious pilgrimages to the Luther sites in Worms, Wittenberg, Eisenach, Eisleben and Leipzig were cultivated. Because most of the sites were in the East, over 250,000 tourists traveled to the restored sites in the German Democratic Republic that coveted hard currency and international respectability.[73] For the 500th Anniversary of the Reformation a reunited Germany has invested enormous sums into the museums and landmarks of the Reformation and planned a decade-long observance with each year featuring a different theme of the Reformation. This will culminate in a celebration in 2017. The 2017 event will again be celebrated with church and cultural events, conferences, and large exhibitions that will now be ecumenical and global.[74]

---

conjunction with the Martin Luther Jubilee in Washington, D.C. See "All Saints Sunday Bulletin, November 6, 1983, LCA Weekly Church Bulletins, © 1983 by the Board of Publication of the Lutheran Church in America. See also, *The Lutheran* 21/19 (November 2, 1983) 3.

72. Hoelterhoff, "East Germans Get Religion for Luther 500th."

73. Ibid.

74. See Lehmann, *Luthergedächtnis 1817 bis 2017*. The themes have been and will be the following: 2009 Reformation and Confession with a focus on Calvin and the Barmen Declaration; 2010 Reformation and Education with a focus on Melanchthon and the educational impulses of the Reformation; 2011 Reformation and Freedom with a focus on the righteous path under the guidance of God's word and solidarity and concern for one's neighbor; 2012 Reformation and Music with a focus on the Reformation's foundational contribution to European music—Bach, Schutz, Telemann and Handel; 2013 Reformation and Tolerance with a focus on the 450th anniversary of the Council of Trent and the 40th anniversary of the Leuenberg Agreement as a witness to Protestant ecumenism; 2014 Reformation and Politics with a focus on Authority and personal responsibility, faith and power, freedom of conscience and human rights; 2015 Reformation-Visual Arts and Bible with a focus on Cranach the Younger, the media and language revolution during the Reformation; 2016 Reformation and the One World with a focus on the Reformation's global influence as its message spread in the world to more than 400 million Protestants; 2017 Anniversary of the Reformation with a focus on the celebration of worldwide church and cultural events, conferences, large exhibitions—the climax of the Luther Decade but not the end of encounters with Luther's life and works. "500 Years of the Reformation; Theme Years of the Luther Decade."

Towards the Commemoration of 2017

The Lutheran World Federation and the Pontifical Council for Promoting Christian Unity have jointly published the document "From Conflict to Communion" to affirm that the commemoration of the Reformation in 2017 will be the first to be celebrated in a global and ecumenical age. The writers of "From Conflict to Communion" note that the commemoration of 2017 will be a celebration and a call to repentance for our role in the division of the church among other failures. This call to repentance is certainly faithful to Martin Luther's theme in the Ninety-Five Theses.

Without starting a regular tradition of Reformation day observances, the seventeenth century observance of October 31 in 1617 was in part a defensive celebration of Lutheranism's confessional identity as a movement in the church catholic towards the development of a church its own right. Given fewer external threats to its existence the eighteenth-century commemoration in 1717 was a more confident while still unfocused celebration of Protestantism and the enlightenment. With objections from confessionalists, the nineteenth century observances both in 1817 and 1883 pulled out all the stops for a celebration to identify Luther and Lutheranism with the newness that Protestantism represented and its continued contributions to freedom, liberalism and progress. The twentieth century confronted the commemorations with profound ambiguities. While wanting to celebrate, two world wars primarily among Christian nations, genocide whatever its multiple causes in the lands where Lutheranism at first prospered, and secularism which began to empty churches of worshippers sobered the organizers. Att the same time hopeful steps towards ecumenical conversations began.

The celebration of the Ninety-Five Theses at the centennial intervals started out without much fanfare and grew to dramatic and triumphalistic events when Protestantism was at its height and represented for itself and cultures the fresh springs of modernism. The chords of progress, liberalism, and especially in Germany nationalism and the formation of the German nation were struck only to wane again as scholars began to blend Luther and the Reformation into the wider history of reform. Church leaders began to focus on ecumenical dialog, and the culture dictated a decline of denominational identity.

For the 500th anniversary of the nailing of the Ninety-Five Theses, Martin Luther the Catholic Reformer, who was excommunicated from his church and pronounced a heretic, has become the catholic reformer that he felt called to be. He has not only been claimed by Protestants the world over as a renewer of the faith but also reclaimed by the Roman Catholic Church as a Doctor of the Church by accepting his theological proposals to be within the bounds of catholic theology. The communion that bears his name has begun to see its theological and interim contribution as a bridge for reconciliation among the churches with a vison for the unity for which Christ prayed.

Bibliography

Böhmer, Heinrich. *Luther in the Light of Recent Research*. Translated by Carl F. Huth Jr. Published for the New York Reformation Quadricentenary Committee. New York: Christian Herald, 1916.

Bornkamm, Heinrich. *Thesen und Thesenanschlag Luthers: Geschehen und Bedeutung*. Theologische Bibliothek Töpelmann 14. Berlin: Töplelman, 1967.

The Common Service Book, 1917 of the Lutheran Church. Philadelphia: Board of Publication of the United Lutheran Church in America, 1917.

Dűrr, Alfred. *The Cantatas of J. S. Bach*. 2nd ed. Translated by Richard Jones. Oxford: Oxford University Press, 2005.

Granquist, Mark. *A New History: Lutherans in America*. Minneapolis: Fortress, 2015.

Gritsch, Eric W. *Martin Luther's Anti-Semistism: Against His Better Judgment*. Grand Rapids: Eerdmans, 2012.

Hendrix, Scott. "American Luther Research in the Twentieth Century." *Lutheran Quarterly* 25.1 (2001) 1–23.

Howard, Thomas Albert. "Remembering the Reformation, 1817 and 1883: Commemorating the Past as Agent and Mirror of Social Change," in *Religion and Innovation: Antagonists or Partners*, edited by Donald Yerxa. London: Bloomsbury Arcadia, 2016.

Howard, Thomas Albert, and Mark Noll, "The Reformation at Five Hundred." *First Things* (November 2014) 43–48.

Huovinen, Eero. "Doctor communis? The Ecumenical Significance of Martin Luther's Theology." In *Lutheranism Legacy and Future: Essays in Honor of Eric W. Gritsch*, edited by Holger Roggelin and Scott Gustafson. 136–53. West Conshohocken, PA: Infinity, 2010.

Kaufmann, Thomas. *A Short Life of Martin Luther*. Translated by Peter D. S. Krey and James D. Bratt. Grand Rapids: Eerdmans, 2017.

Kolb, Robert. *Martin Luther as Prophet, Teacher, Hero: Images of the Reformer 1520–1620*. Grand Rapids: Baker, 1999.

Landry, Stan M. *Ecumenism, Memory, and German Nationalism 1817–1917*. Syracuse: Syracuse University Press, 2014.

Lehmann, Hartmut. *Luthergedächtnis 1817 bis 2017*. Refo500 Academic Studies 8. Göttingen: Vandenhoeck & Ruprecht, 2012.

Leppin, Volker, and Timothy J. Wengert. "Sources for and against the Posting of the Ninety-Five Theses." *Lutheran Quarterly* 29 (2015) 373–98.

Lohse, Bernard. *Martin Luther: An Introduction to His Life and Work*. Translated by Robert C. Schultz. Philadelphia: Fortress, 1986.

Lund, Eric. *Documents from the History of Lutheranism, 1517–1750*. Philadelphia: Fortress, 2002.

Luther, Martin. *D. Martin Luthers Werke, Kritisch Gesamtausgabe*: [*Schriften*]. 73 vols. Weimar: Böhlaus, 1883–2009.

———. *D. Martin Luthers Werke, Kritische Gesamtausgabe: Briefwechsel*. 18 vols. Weimar: Böhlaus, 1930–1983.

Manns, Peter, and Jeroslav Pelikan. *Martin Luther: An Illustrated Biography*. New York: Crossroad, 1982.

Nelson, E. Clifford. *The Lutherans in North America*. Philadelphia: Fortress, 1975.

Oberman, Heiko. *Forerunners of the Reformation: The Shape of Late Medieval Thought Illustrated by Key Documents*. Philadelphia: Fortress, 1981.

———. *The Dawn of the Reformation: Essays in Late Medieval and Early Reformation Thought*. Edinburgh: T. & T. Clark, 1986.

Pecklers, Keith F., and Brian D. Spinks, "The Liturgical Movement." In *The New Westminster Dictionary of Liturgy and Worship*, edited by Paul Bradshaw, 283–89. Louisville: Westminster John Knox, 2002.

Pelikan, Jeroslav. *Bach among the Theologians*. 1986. Reprint, Eugene, OR: Wipf & Stock, 2003.

———, ed. *Interpreters of Luther: Essays in Honor of Wilhelm Pauck*. Philadelphia: Fortress, 1968.

———. *Obedient Rebels: Catholic Substance and Protestant Principle in Luther's Reformation*. New York: Harper & Row, 1964.

Piepkorn, Arthur Karl. "A Lutheran Theologian looks at the Ninety-Five Theses in 1967." *Theological Studies* 28/3 (September, 1967) 519–30.

Schaff, Philip. *History of the Christian Church*. Vol. 5. 2nd ed. New York: Scribner, 1892.

Schjorring, Jens Holger, Prassnna Kumari and Norman A. Hjelm, editors. *From Federation to Communion: The History of the Lutheran World Federation*. Minneapolis: Fortress, 1997.

Stephens, Barry. *Performing the Reformation in the City of Luther*. Oxford: Oxford University Press, 2010.

Stiller, Günther. *Johann Sebastian Bach and Liturgical Life in Leipzig*. St. Louis: Concordia, 1984.

Wendebourg, Dorothea. "Vergangene Reformationsjubiläen: Ein Rückblick im Vorfeld von 2017." In *Der Reformator Martin Luther 2017*, edited by Heinz Schilling, 261–81. Berlin : de Gruyter Oldenbourg, 2014.

Wilkens, Robert. "Lutheran Pietism and Catholic Piety." In *The Catholicity of the Reformation*, edited by Carl E. Braaten and Robert W. Jenson, 79–92. Grand Rapids: Eerdmans, 1996.

2

Martin Luther and the Episcopal Church

—Robert W. Prichard

One would have good ground to argue there is no place in this collection of essays for a discussion of the observance in the Episcopal Church and other churches of the Anglican Communion of anniversaries commemorating the critical role of Martin Luther in the Protestant Reformation. Simply put, such commemorations have been almost nonexistent in the history of Anglicanism. Nevertheless, the Lutheran and Anglican Churches are currently in close relation with one another and have a shared history of cooperation that extends back to the early years of the Reformation.

Rather than tracing anniversary celebration in the years of 1517, 1617, 1717, 1817, 1917, and 2017, this essay will use those years as symbolic markers to trace that often close relationship of Anglicans and Lutherans. The essay will point to both high and low points in that relationship and will in the process ponder the question as to why Anglicans have not been more active in their celebration of relationship to and indebtedness to the Lutheran churches.

1517

There is no question that the spark that began the English Reformation was lit in Wittenberg. Within five years of the Ninety-Five theses, scholars at

Cambridge and elsewhere in England were studying Lutheran texts.[1] An important early group met at the White Horse Tavern in Cambridge; their theological preferences were well enough known that their critics began to call the inn "Little Germany."[2] Historians of the Reformation have not been able to date the precise year in which such discussion began, but A. G. Dickens's observation that it must have been prior to the first public burning of Luther's works in late 1520 or early 1521 is certainly suggestive.[3]

English contact with the reform of the continent was not limited to the reading of Lutheran works. William Tyndale (1494–1536), an Oxford graduate who may or may not have participated in the White Horse Inn, travelled to Wittenberg in 1524 in order to meet Luther.[4] Robert Barnes (c. 1495–1540), the prior of the Augustinian Friars in Cambridge, took up residence in Wittenberg in 1528, and served as a go-between in negotiations between Lutheran princes and Henry VIII for much of the following decade.[5] In 1532 future Archbishop of Canterbury Thomas Cranmer (1489–1556), sent to Germany by Henry VIII to solicit support for the king's campaign to divorce Catherine of Aragon, spent considerable time in Nuremberg with Lutheran Reformer Andreas Osiander (1489–1552). Cranmer would marry the niece of Osiander's wife's in the summer of that year.[6]

Many of the early supporters of the Reformation in England down played their connections with the Lutheran Reformation. They did so for good reason. English monarch Henry VIII had received the title "Defender of the Faith" for his authorship or patronage of the *Assertio Septem Sacramentorum* (1521), a renunciation of Luther's doctrine of the Sacraments in the *Babylonian Captivity of the Church* (1520). Henry was, moreover,

---

1. A. G. Dickens suggested that the circle of scholars at Cambridge meeting to study Luther's works "could have begun before the year 1520." Claire Cross suggested that "Lutheranism had penetrated into the country from the Continent for almost a decade before the Reformation Parliament first assembled" in 1529. Gilley and Sheils suggest that this happened "from 1520." Euan Cameron put the beginning of the Reformation in English Reformation slightly later, sometime "early in the 1520s." See Dickens, *The English Reformation*, 91; Cross, *Church and People: England 1450–1660*, 42; Gilley et al., *A History of Religion in Britain*, 154; and Cameron, *The European Reformation*, 280.

2 MacCulloch, *Thomas Cranmer*, 25.

3. Dickens, *English Reformation*, 91.

4. Ibid., 93.

5. *Encyclopaedia Britannica Online*, s. v. "Robert Barnes." http://www.britannica.com/biography/Robert-Barnes.

6. MacCulloch, *Thomas Cranmer*, 70–71.

irritated by Martin Luther's objection to his plans for divorcing Catherine of Aragon.[7] Henry did warm to some Lutheran ideas in the middle of the 1530s, but after his failed marriage with Anne of Cleves in 1540 the monarch turned his ire against Lutheran ideas once again, having his ambassador to Germany (Robert Barnes) burned at the stake for heresy.[8]

It is not surprising, therefore, that early English Protestants sought to explain the source of their religious ideas without reference to Luther. Thomas Bilney (1495–1531), one of the earliest of the Cambridge scholars to be attracted to Reformation ideas, is a case in point. Chronicler John Foxe later published excerpts from a series of five letters that Bilney wrote to humanist bishop Cuthbert Tunstall (1474–1559). Bilney explained to the bishop that he had come to a new understanding of the Gospel. Bilney compared himself to the woman with the flow of blood in Mark 5:25–34 who spent all she had on physicians without getting any better. Bilney said that he used up his strength, his money, and his wit following the advice of "unlearned hearers of confession" who "appointed . . . fasting, watching, buying of pardons, and masses." He concluded that they did so more for "their own gain, than the salvation of [his] sick and languishing soul."[9] The reading of 1 Timothy freed him from his plight. Bilney explained to Tunstall:

> At the first reading (as I well remember) I chanced upon this sentence of St. Paul (O most sweet and comfortable sentence to my soul!) in 1 Tim. 15., "It is a true saying and worthy of all men to be embraced, that Christ Jesus came into the world to save sinners; of whom I am the chief and principal." This one sentence through God's instruction and inward working, which I did not then perceive did so exhilarate my heart, being wounded with the guilt of my sins, and being almost in despair, that immediately I felt a marvelous comfort and quietness, insomuch "that my bruised bones leaped for joy."[10]

The key verse in 1 Timothy that Bilney identified was one that that Luther had cited multiple times in his pivotal 1513–15 *Lectures on the Psalms*.[11] In his later Commentary on 1 Timothy, Luther identified this

---

7. Ibid., 65.
8. Dickens, *English Reformation*, 202.
9. Foxe, *The Acts*, 6.
10. Ibid., 635.
11. LW, vol. 10: *First Lectures on the Psalms I, Chapters1–75*, 34, 123, 163, 233, 239.

passage as "the text by which Paul himself was saved," and as a passage that "has quite often been life and salvation for" him.[12] An objective observer might logically see a link between Bilney's discovery and Luther's teaching. Yet Bilney made no reference to the Lutheran books that had been circulated and discussed at Cambridge. Rather he gave all the credit to humanist Desiderius Erasmus (1466–1536), who had taught at Cambridge from 1511 to 14 and had issued a new Latin translation of the New Testament, with editions in 1516 and 1519. Not incidentally. Erasmus was respected by Bishop Tunstall and by King Henry VIII. Luther was not.

By the middle of the sixteenth century, English Protestants were inclined to overlook Lutheran influence for a second reason: increasing ties with the Reformed Church. Efforts by the English to bring such Lutheran scholars as Andreas Osiander and Philip Melanchthon (1497–1560) were unsuccessful.[13] In contrast Reformed theologians Martin Bucer (1491–1551) and Peter Martyr Vermigli (1499–1562) accepted teaching positions at Cambridge and Oxford, and the Reformed cities of Geneva and Zurich hosted significant groups of English exiles during the reign of Queen Mary I.

It would not be until the middle of the nineteenth century that Anglican historian Charles Hardwick (1821–59) would show how deeply the Church of England was influenced by the Lutheran Reformation. In his *History of the Articles of Religion* (1851), Hardwick demonstrated that the Augsburg Confession

> contributed directly, in no inconsiderable degree, to the construction of the public Formularies of Faith approved by the Church of England. The XIII. Articles, drawn up, it would seem, in 1538, were almost entirely based upon the language of the Germanic Confession; while the same sort of respect is no less apparent in the Articles of Edward VI., and consequently in those which are now binding on the whole body of the clergy [The Articles of Religion].[14]

During the sixteenth century, English Protestants were more likely to acknowledge the humanistic and Reformed influences on their church

---

12. Luther, LW, vol. 28: *Commentaries on 1 Corinthians 7, 1 Corinthians 15, Lectures on 1 Timothy*, 246.

13. MacCulloch, *Thomas Cranmer*, 71, 240–63, and 539.

14. Hardwick, *A History of the Articles of Religion*, 32.

than they were to acknowledge connections to the Lutheran Reformation, often as simply a matter of survival.

1617

At the time of the first centenary of the Ninety-Five Theses, leaders of the Anglican, Lutheran, and Reformed Church were acutely aware of the need for ecumenical cooperation. Roman Catholic powers—Spain, Portugal, France, and Austria—were dominating Europe and, in the case of the first three of the four nations, establishing colonies and missions outside of Europe. The dynastic changes that would spark the Thirty Years War began in 1617 with the decision of the Spanish to support Ferdinand II to follow the aging and childless Matthias as King of Bohemia, Archduke of Austria, King of Hungary and Croatia, and Holy Roman Emperor, positions Ferdinand assumed in the years from 1617 to 1619, the year when Matthias died.[15] Ferdinand's uncompromising attempt to impose Roman Catholicism on his subjects would soon spark a war that would encompass most of Europe.

Anglican scholar Norman Sykes explained the situation of Protestants in this way:

> Both the ecclesiastical and political aspects of the struggle against Rome need to be borne in mind, for they were two facets of the same shield of defense. But it is not just on the one hand to argue that the ecclesiastical relationship sprang solely from the political exigency, nor on the other to ignore the difficult questions arising from the yoking together of the diverse Protestant churches, differing in ecclesiastical polity and order yet united in common hostility to Rome. Ecclesiastical grand alliances, like their political counterparts, have their internal stresses and tensions; and the Protestant front had to face the novel problem of the diversities of church government between Anglican, Lutheran and Reformed churches.[16]

In his essay on this "Protestant front," Sykes focused primarily on the question of church order but noted Protestant attempts at theological accord as well. One of the key examples that he cited was the Synod of Dort,

---

15. *Encyclopedia Britannica Online*, s. v. "Ferdinand II." http://www.britannica.com/biography/Ferdinand-II-Holy-Roman-emperor.
16. Sykes, *The Church of England*, 3–4.

which met from the fall of 1618 to the spring of 1619. Although primarily remembered as a gathering of Reformed Christians, there were also Lutheran representatives from Bremen, representatives from the Church of England, and representatives from the Church of Scotland. The deputations from England and Scotland (separate countries that had shared a single monarch since the death of Queen Elizabeth I) sent by King James I of England/James VI of Scotland included the future Bishop of Norfolk Joseph Hall (1574–1656).[17] When the session convened on November 13, 1618, approximately one hundred delegates, of whom one-third were from outside Holland, were present.[18] Hall would later optimistically summarize the relationship of the Protestant Churches represented at Dort in this way:

> Blessed be God, there is no difference in any essential matter betwixt the Church of England and her sisters of the Reformation. We accord in every point of Christian doctrine, without the least variation; their public Confessions and ours are sufficient convictions to the world of our full and absolute agreement.[19]

One concrete manifestation of this perception of shared interest was evident on the ground in Western Hemisphere, where a string of small Protestant colonies—Virginia (1607), New Netherland (1614), New England (1620), and New Sweden (1638)—were clustered together on the eastern coast of North America, surrounded by claims to larger portions of territory by the French and Spanish to the North, West, and South.

The political cooperation of these Protestant colonies ended with the New Netherland's annexing New Sweden in 1655 and with the English taking New Netherland in 1674. Perceptions of shared religious interest would persist, however. As historian John Woolverton has noted in his *Colonial Anglican in North America*, Anglican clergy in the colonies saw "German and Swedish Lutherans, Dutch Calvinist, [and] French Huguenots" as fellow Protestant Christians and made a "modest attempt to incorporate them in the lay ranks" of the Church of England.[20] This happened most frequently, but not solely, at the point in which colonists of those traditions switched their worship from their native tongues into the English language.

17. Scott, *The Articles of the Synod of Dort*, 165 and 197.

18. González, *The Story of Christianity*, vol. 2: *The Reformation to the Present Day*, 181.

19. John Hall, *Works*, 8:58, cited in Sykes, *Church of England and Non-Episcopal Churches*, 23.

20. Woolverton, *Colonial Anglicanism in North America*, 25.

While Joseph Hall had noted that Anglicans shared a common faith with Lutheran and Reformed Churches, which he counted as the "sisters of the Reformation," he did note a "difference in the form of outward administration"—i.e. in church order. Hall argued that the difference in polity was "not to be essential to the being of a church, though much importing the well or better being of it, according to our several apprehensions thereof."[21] It mattered to him, nonetheless, as the title of his later volume *Episcopacy by Divine Right* (1640) suggested.

The concern for church order led Hall and other high-church Anglicans to favor the Lutheran Churches over the Reformed Churches. Archbishop of Canterbury William Laud (1573–1645) asked those who argued that "all of the Reformed Kirks" had abandoned the episcopacy at the Reformation whether they:

> be so strait-laced as not to admit the churches of Sweden and Denmark, and indeed all or most of the Lutherans, to be reformed churches? For in Sweden they retained both the thing [episcopacy] and the name: and the governors of their churches are, and are called, bishops. And among other Lutherans, the thing is retained, though not the name. For instead of bishops, they are called superintendents, and instead of archbishops, general superintendents. And yet even here too these names differ more in sound than in sense. For bishop is the same in Greek, that superintendent is in Latin. Nor is this change very well-liked by the learned. Howsoever, Luther since he would change the name, did yet very wisely, that he would leave the thing, and make choice of such a name as was not altogether unknown to the ancient church.[22]

Laud would not be the only Anglican author to opine that "the learned" among the Lutherans favored the retention of the episcopacy; such claims would become a standard high-church Anglican characterization of Lutheran attitudes. For example, Herbert Thorndike (1598–1672) would write in a work published in 1670 that "it appeareth sufficiently that very many learned and religious persons of those [Lutheran] churches have not only approved the episcopacy here settled, but wished the benefit of it to themselves."[23]

---

21. Joseph Hall, *Works*, 7:58, cited in Sykes, *Church of England*, 23.
22. Laud, Works (L.A.C.T.) 3:386, cited in Sykes, *Church of England*, 16.
23. Thorndike, "A Discourse of the Forbearance of the Penalties," 5:429.

This characterization—whether accurate or not—enabled Anglicans to hold positive attitudes toward Lutherans in the post-English Civil War period in which the Church of England became increasingly critical of Christians of the Reformed tradition, who had temporarily suspended episcopacy from the Church of England in the Interregnum.

1717

At the time of the second centennial of the Ninety-Five Theses, George I, a German Lutheran occupied the throne of the United Kingdom (created by the Acts of Union of Act of 1706–7 that united England and Scotland into one kingdom). George I was, therefore, the "Supreme Governor of the Church of England," a title that English monarchs have claimed since the time of Queen Elizabeth I.[24] His Protestant faith was the reason for his accession to the English throne. After the attempts of James II (King of England, 1685–88) to restore the Roman Catholic Church in England and the resultant Glorious Revolution (1688) in which James II was driven from the throne, the English Parliament had adopted the Bill of Rights of 1689, which included the following provision:

> And whereas it hath been found by experience that it is inconsistent with the safety and welfare of this Protestant kingdom to be governed by a popish prince, or by any king or queen marrying a papist, the said Lords Spiritual and Temporal and Commons do further pray that it may be enacted, that all and every person and persons that is, are or shall be reconciled to or shall hold communion with the see or Church of Rome, or shall profess the popish religion, or shall marry a papist, shall be excluded and be forever incapable to inherit, possess or enjoy the crown and government of this realm and Ireland and the dominions thereunto belonging or any part of the same, or to have, use or exercise any regal power, authority or jurisdiction within the same; and in all and every such case or cases the people of these realms shall be and are hereby absolved of their allegiance; and the said crown and government shall from time to time descend to and be enjoyed by such person or persons being Protestants as should have inherited and enjoyed the same in case the said person or persons so reconciled, holding

---

24. Elizabeth's father Henry VIII and brother Edward VI had claimed the less nuanced title of "Supreme Head of the Church of England."

communion or professing or marrying as aforesaid were naturally dead.²⁵

This provision cut off the line of succession for James II and the son of his second marriage, who were Roman Catholics. Significantly, it required later monarchs to be Protestants but did not specify the Church of England. Monarchs were expected, however, to receive communion in the Church of England on an occasional basis, an action that was viewed as recognizing the legitimacy of the Church of England. This provision was incorporated in the Act of Settlement of 1700, which directed that "whosoever shall hereafter come to the Possession of this Crown shall joyn in Communion with the Church of England as by Law established."²⁶

It was this provision for a Protestant monarch had made it possible for Georg Ludwig (1660–1727), Prince Elector of Hanover to become King George I of England in 1714. He was not, however, the first non-Anglican Protestant to occupy the English throne. After James II was ejected from the monarchy, the English Parliament had turned to the two daughters from James's first marriage, Mary and Anne, as his successors to the throne. Both were married to Protestants: Mary to William, Prince of Orange, who was a Reformed Christian, and Anne to Prince George of Denmark, who was a Lutheran. William (king, 1789–1702) shared the throne jointly with his wife Mary (queen 1789–1694), until Mary's death. George of Denmark, who had been limited from exercising authority in England by his not always friendly brother-in-law, was not accorded the same joint rule with his wife Anne (queen, 1702–17), though he had been made Duke of Cumberland by the Parliament in 1689.

George was more consistent in his attachment to his non-Anglican Protestantism than was William. He maintained a circle of Lutheran friends and a Lutheran royal chapel at the Court of St. James.²⁷ The court opened the door to conversation between Anglicans and Lutherans, particularly in regard to foreign mission and mission and to Pietism. The first Danish Lutheran chaplain, J. W. Meckin, attended meetings of the Society for the Promoting Christian Knowledge (SPCK), the first Anglican missionary

---

25. "English Bill of Rights 1689," Yale Law School, Lillian Goldman Law Library, The Avlaon Project, http://avalon.law.yale.edu/17th_century/england.asp.

26. The National Archives, "Act of Settlement (1700)," 1700 CHAPTER 2 12 and 13 Will 3, http://www.legislation.gov.uk/aep/Will3/12-13/2.

27. Sirota, *The Christian Monitors*, 138.

society, from the year after its founding in 1698.[28] His successor as chaplain, Anton Wilhelm Boehm, joined the SPCK. He published an English translation of Lutheran Pietist A. H. Francke's *Fußstapfen* (Footsteps) in 1705 under the English title *Pietas Hallensis*; the work was an early source of Pietist influence in England. He also translated and the SPCK published in 1709, *The Propagation of the Gospel in the East*, an account of the Lutheran mission in India that had been published in German as *Merkwürdige Nachricht* (Notable News) a year earlier. The publication aroused sufficient interest that the SPCK began to contribute to the support of Danish-sponsored German Lutheran missionaries in Tranquebar in India.[29]

George I came to the English throne in 1714, because neither William and Mary, nor Anne and George had any had children who survived them. George benefitted from the earlier experiences of William III and George of Denmark. There already was a Lutheran presence in London when George arrived. Anton William Boehm, for example, continued as Lutheran chaplain, becoming what SPCK secretary Henry Newman would characterize at his 1722 funeral as "the life and soul or our correspondence in religious affairs with Germany and Denmark."[30]

Lutherans were of mixed minds about the wisdom of trans-denominational Protestant dynastic marriages. The issue was not confined to England. Lutheran-Reformed and Lutheran Roman Catholic royal unions were a matter of debate in Germany. Some Lutheran divines, such as Franke, argued against attempts by monarchs to reconcile two different religious traditions, while others such as Gottfried Wilhelm Leibniz (1646–1716) and Daniel Ernst Jablonski (1660–1741), were supportive of the idea.[31]

Anglicans were of divided minds about the broader prospects of cooperation, as well. Archbishop Thomas Tenison (Archbishop of Canterbury, 1694–1715) was critical, for example, of the SPCK support of Lutheran missionaries in India, though supportive of the accession of George I.[32] His successor, William Wake (Archbishop of Canterbury, 1715–37) engaged in what historian Norman Sykes called "a long and earnest correspondence with representatives of foreign Protestant churches, both Lutheran and Reformed," and "explicitly and formally authorized the practice of inter-

---

28. Ibid., 138.
29. Roberts, *Converting Colonialism*, 2:238.
30. Henry Newman quoted in Sirota, *Christian Monitors*, 138.
31. Schunka, "Mixed Matches and Inter-Confessional Dialogue," 139–44.
32. Sirota, *Christian Monitors*, 140.

communion between the Church of England and Lutheran and Reformed churches in regard to the members of each church sojourning in the territory of the other."[33]

Anglican-Lutheran discussion became wrapped up in the broader discussion of Anglican-Lutheran-Reformed relationships. In 1722 George I and Frederick William I of Prussia invited representatives of the Protestant Churches of thirty-nine different jurisdictions in Europe to a discussion in Ratisbon about the possibility of church union. Despite the support of Archbishop Wake and Jablonski, the effort fizzled due in large part to George's concern about rising Prussian influence within Germany. Historian Norman Sykes suggests that the failure of the conference led to the fading of "the hopes of Protestant union." Further, Sykes suggested, "the Church of England drifted out of close relationship with the Lutheran and Reformed churches of Europe for more than a century and a half."[34]

Sykes did offer an exception to his characterization of the end of close relationship, a shared effort in the Middle East in the mid-nineteenth century that will be mentioned later in this essay. He could well also have included the experience in colonial North America where Anglican and Lutheran clergy and laity remained on generally good terms, especially in Pennsylvania and North Carolina, where there were concentrations of Lutheran immigrants.

Anglican and Swedish Lutherans were engaged in occasional pulpit exchanges in Pennsylvania from the 1720s, a far closer relationship than either church had with churches of the Reformed tradition. Swedish Lutheran clergyman Andrew Rudman (1668–1708) characterized cooperation in this way: "We have always been counseled and instructed from Sweden to maintain friendship and unity with the English, so that we and the English Church shall not reckon each other as dissenters like the Presbyterians, Anabaptist, Quakers, &c., but as Sister Churches."[35] At mid-century Anglican clergy such as William Smith (1727–1803) and Richard Peters (1704–1776) of Philadelphia were hopeful to extend such cordial relationships to include the growing number of German Lutherans in Pennsylvania. They communicated with members of the nonsectarian German Society in the colony and about union of the two churches. Smith even wrote to England reunion was something that he was "sure would easily take effect" given

---

33. Sykes, *The Church of England*, 33–34.
34. Sykes, *Daniel Ernest Jablonski and the Church of England*, 30–31.
35. Andrew Rudman quoted in Gough, "The Colonial Church," 33.

the right circumstances. In the following decade Smith was joined in his hope by Anglican missionary Thomas Barton (1730–1780), who wrote to the Society for the Propagation of the Gospel (SPG, founded in 1701 to support salaries of clergy in foreign mission) in 1766 that Lutheran clergy frequently were proposing "a union with the Church of England" in their clergy gatherings. Smith seconded that sentiment in a separate letter in the same year.[36]

Later in the century Episcopalians in North Carolina were involved in an interesting ecumenical arrangement with Lutherans. Episcopalians in the state had not yet succeeded in establishing the episcopate and therefore were unable to ordain needed clergy. They turned to the Lutherans who in 1794 ordained Robert Johnson Miller (1758–1834) a presbyter with the understanding that he would serve Episcopal congregations. For the next twenty-seven years Miller served as a advocate of unity between Lutherans and Episcopalians and was active in both the Lutheran Synod and the Episcopal Convention. Unable to bring about such a union, he accepted re-ordination in the Episcopal Church in 1821.

1817

In the year 1817 an energetic clergyman by the name of William Holland Wilmer (1782–1827) was elected president of the Episcopal Church's House of Deputies—the highest position of authority available for a presbyter in the polity of the Episcopal Church. He was at the time deeply involved in an attempt to revive the Episcopal Church in Virginia. In the following six years he would create a theological journal (*The Washington Theological Repertory*, 1819–28), publish a theological text (*The Episcopal Manual*, 1822), play a leading role in the founding of a theological seminary (The Protestant Episcopal Theological Seminary in Virginia, 1823), and serve as that seminary's first professor. Two convictions lay at the heart of his many efforts: (1) the belief that Episcopalians needed to claim their heritage as a church of the Reformation and (2) a recognition that Episcopalians who shared his convictions could learn something from the successful efforts of John Henry Hobart (1775–1830) to create and nurture a high-church party for the Episcopal Church.[37] Thus, in the place of a high-church emphasis

---

36. Ibid., 34.

37. For a description of Hobart's efforts see Mullin, *Episcopal Vision/American Reality*.

on episcopal ordination as the guarantor of a valid ministry, Wilmer and his allies in a growing evangelical Episcopal party stressed the importance of personal faith and fidelity to Scripture. Luther, under appreciated by Episcopalians who stressed the necessity of the episcopacy for church order, played a more important role in Wilmer's narrative.

Volume 1, number one of the *Washington Theological Repertory*, sounded a note that would be repeated in an article, John Wickliffe. Wickliffe was to be appreciated because his teaching "prepared the minds of men for that great and glorious reformation in religion which was afterwards effected by Martin Luther."[38] The following year, number 12 of the same volume carried an extended article on justification. It cited Luther in explaining justification: "the doctrine of justification by faith is termed by Luther, the distinguishing characteristic of a rising or falling church."[39]

Anglicans and Lutherans continued the cooperation in World mission that dated from the mission in Tranquebar, India. The newly founded Church Missionary Society (CMS, 1799) initially drew its missionaries almost exclusively from among German Lutherans.[40] Important early work among the Tamil-speaking was carried on for the CMS from 1820 to 1835, for example, by Lutheran pastor Charles T. E. Rhenius (1790–1838). When Anglicans ordained their first native Indian priest, it would be a man (Gnanamuthu Devasagaiyam, deacon 1847, priest 1849) "in all probability brought up under the teachings of Lutheran pietists."[41]

It was in Jerusalem that Anglicans and Lutherans engaged in their most ambitious ecumenical enterprise. In 1841 Christian Charles Josias von Bunsen (1791–1860), a German theologian and diplomat who served as Frederick William IV of Prussia minister in London (1841–54), proposed a joint Anglican-Lutheran bishopric for the Middle East to be located in Jerusalem. The idea, which was accepted by the English King and Parliament, was for a bishop, chosen alternatively from the Anglicans and Lutherans, who would preside over a diocese whose clergy agreed to either the Augsburg Confession or to the English Articles of Religion and Book of Common Prayer. The first bishop selected was a Jewish convert to Anglicanism and Hebrew scholar by the name of Michael Solomon Alexander

---

38. Miscellaneous Department, "The Life of John Wickliffe," 42.
39. Ibid., 42.
40. Williams, "British Religion and the Wider World," 384.
41. Moffett, *History of Christianity in Asia*, 2:268–69.

(1799–1845).⁴² He was followed by Samuel Gobat (1799–1879), a Lutheran pastor who had served for a time with the Church Missionary Society. After the short episcopate of Irish Anglican Joseph Barclay (1831–81) the Prussian-English agreement lapsed, and Lutherans and Anglicans began to pursue their efforts separately.

Some members of the high-church "Oxford Movement" objected strongly to the Jerusalem Episcopate. By some accounts it was the creation of the episcopate there that led Oxford Movement leader John Henry Newman (1801–1890) to leave the Church of England for the Roman Catholic Church. Newman regarded Lutheranism and Calvinism as "heresies, repugnant to Scripture, springing up three centuries since, and anathematized by East as well as West."⁴³

The high-church party's stress on episcopacy and—in cases like Newman—total rejection of non-Episcopal ministry made broad ecumenical conversation with Lutherans difficult. Members of the Episcopal Church and other Anglicans were, however, occasionally able to focus on discussion with the Scandinavian Lutheran Churches, because they had retained episcopacy at the Reformation. In 1856, therefore, the Episcopal Church's General Convention would establish a "Committee on Friendly Intercourse with the Church in Sweden."⁴⁴ The Lambeth Conference, the decennial meeting of Anglican Bishops that began in the 1850s, followed suit, calling for discussion with Swedish Lutherans in 1897 and 1908.⁴⁵ So long, however, as members of the high-church party opposed discussions with those Lutherans who lacked episcopal succession, it was difficult for the two denominations to hold communion-wide conversations.

1917

World War I limited the degree to which Christians were able to engage in ecumenical discussion. The 1920 Lambeth Conference, which would have met two years earlier, had not been for the war, returned to the discussion

---

42. Bowen, *the Idea of the Victorian Church*, 75–77.

43. John Henry Newman quoted in Bowen, *Idea of the Victorian Church*, 77.

44. Church records are not entirely consistent about the name of the committee. This form of the name appears in the *Journal* of the 1871 General Convention. See *Journal of the Proceedings of the Bishops, the Clergy and the Laity of the Protestant Episcopal Church*, 381

45. Markham, et al. "The Lambeth Conference," 98.

of Anglican Lutheran relationships that had occupied the two previous sessions. Resolution 24 of the 1920 Conference welcomed

> the Report of the Commission appointed after the last Conference entitled "The Church of England and the Church of Sweden," and, accepting the conclusions there maintained on the succession of bishops of the Church of Sweden and the conception of the priesthood set forth in its standards, recommends that members of that Church, qualified to receive the sacrament in their own Church, should be admitted to Holy Communion in ours. It also recommends that on suitable occasions permission should be given to Swedish ecclesiastics to give addresses in our churches.[46]

The Conference also looked forward to "the event of an invitation being extended to an Anglican bishop or bishops to take part in the consecration of a Swedish bishop." Were such an invitation extended, the conference recommended that, "the invitation should, if possible, be accepted, subject to the approval of the metropolitan."[47]

During the 1920s two movements afoot from earlier in the century that would bear fruit. One was the Faith and Order movement, inspired by an address of Episcopal Bishop Charles Henry Brent (1862–1929) at the World Mission Conference of 1910 in Edinburgh. At a time when many others involved in foreign mission work advocated a careful avoidance of discussion of matters of theology and church order that might prove divisive, Brent favored frank discussion of differences as the logical way forward. Brent promoted the idea tirelessly before, during, and after the war. Near the end of his life, he presided at the first World Conference on Faith and Order in Lausanne Switzerland in 1927. A second movement grew out of the efforts at church cooperation during the war years advanced by Archbishop of Uppsala Nathan Søderblom (1866–1931). His efforts led to convening the first World Conference of Life and Works in 1925. The two movements would join with other bodies in 1947 to form the World Council of Churches.

---

46. Lambeth Conference 1920, Resolution 24, http://www.anglicancommunion.org/resources/document-library/lambeth-conference/1920/resolution-24-reunion-of-christendom?author=Lambeth+Conference&year=1920.

47. Lambeth Conference 1920. Resolution 25, http://www.anglicancommunion.org/resources/document-library/lambeth-conference/1920/resolution-25-reunion-of-christendom?author=Lambeth+Conference&year=1920.

The Episcopal General Convention of 1929 and 1931 began a discussion about church union with Methodists, Presbyterians, and Lutherans.[48] The efforts were not successful. Lutherans in America were otherwise occupied. At one point divided into sixty-six independent church bodies, they focused in final years of World War I on Lutheran reunion.[49] The Methodists withdrew from ecumenical discussion with Episcopalians in order to pursue Methodist reunion. The Episcopal-Presbyterian discussion bogged down in debates about the importance of the episcopacy. Anglican-Lutheran discussion continued at Lambeth Conference, however, with conventions in 1930 and 40 urging the expansion of conversation with Swedish Lutherans to include the other Scandinavian nations, and Finland and Latvia (1930 and 1948).

The creation of the Church of South India in 1947 by uniting the South India United Church (Congregational, Presbyterian, and Reformed), the Anglican missions in Southern India, and the Methodist Church of South India signaled for the first time a possible way forward for Anglicans in discussions about church merger. The Church of South India made a discussion between those who were already ordained (who were accepted as validly ordained clergy, whatever their form of ordination) and future ordinations (which were to be by bishops).

Ecumenical conversations in the 1980s offered language that would prove helpful in mutual recognition of ministry. The World Council of Church's Faith and Order Commission issued *Baptism, Eucharist, and Ministry* (1982) that contrasted *Apostolic Tradition* ("a continuity in apostolic faith, worship and mission has been preserved in churches which have not retained the form of historic episcopate," Ministry 36) with "episcopal succession" ("a sign, though not a guarantee, of continuity and unity of the Church," Ministry 38).

Episcopalians would use this formula in ecumenical discussion with Protestant Churches. The process usually takes three steps. The first is to engage is bi-lateral talks during which the Episcopal Church acknowledges that despite the absence of episcopal succession it recognizes the presence of apostolic tradition in the other church. When those talks reach a sufficient point, the second step is "interim Eucharistic sharing." Episcopalians took that step with the Evangelical Lutheran Church in 1982, and have since done also with the Moravian Church (2003), and the United

---

48. Prichard, *A History of the Episcopal Church*, 270–71.
49 Ahlstrom, *A Religious History of the American People*, 761.

Methodist Church (2006). The final step is full communion, which involves the possibility of the exchange of clergy. The Episcopal Church has reached this step with the Evangelical Lutheran Church ("Called to Common Mission," 1999–2000) and the Moravian Church (2009).

There have been parallel accords elsewhere in the world, including *Porvoo Agreement* of 1996 between British and Irish Anglicans and Nordic and Baltic Lutherans (1996), the Waterloo Declaration of 2001 by the National Convention of the Evangelical Lutheran Church in Canada and the General Synod of the Anglican Church of Canada (2001), and *Covenanting for Mutual Recognition and Reconciliation* between The Anglican Church of Australia and The Lutheran Church of Australia (2001).

One sign of the higher profile of Lutheran-Episcopalians was the decision of the Episcopal Church in 1997 to add Martin Luther's name to the list of Lesser Feasts and Fasts found in the Book of Common Prayer.[50] Another is a cooperative effort in theological education. In 1999 Bexley Hall Divinity School entered a partnership with Trinity Lutheran Seminary of Columbus, Ohio that made it possible for Bexley to offer courses on the Trinity Campus. In 2009 Seabury-Western Seminary in the Chicago area sold its property and made arrangements to offer classes in the headquarters of the Evangelical Lutheran Church in America near Chicago's O'Hare Airport.[51]

2017

The International Anglican-Lutheran International Co-ordinating Committee (ALICC) devoted its 2014 meeting to developing "plans for resources through which Lutherans and Anglicans can commemorate together the year 1517, a moment of greater direct significance for Lutherans, but one which launched a wider reforming movement into wrestling with what it means for the Church to be both catholic and reformed." ALICC indicated that it would encourage Anglicans "to use the resources being produced by the [Lutheran World Federation] in ways that are appropriate for them in their contexts," and said it was "also planning to produce a devotional resource for use by individuals and communities, using ALICC's theological themes: communion in mission and diakonia, within the framework of the

---

50. *General Convention*, 271–72.

51. For information on Bexley Hall and Seabury Western see http://www.bexley-seabury.edu.

LWF themes" for the year 2017, which are "Liberated by God's Grace" and subthemes of "salvation not for sale," "creation not for sale," and "human beings not for sale."[52]

It is not clear at this point whether or how the Episcopal Church will mark the 2017 anniversary on a national level. There is no question, however, that the ELCA and the Episcopal Church are close ecumenical partners with a long shared history.

Bibliography

Ahlstrom, Sydney E. *A Religious History of the American People*. New Haven: Yale University Press, 1972.

Bowen, Desmond. *The Idea of the Victorian Church*. Montreal: McGill University Press, 1968.

Cameron, Euon. *The European Reformation*. Oxford: Clarendon, 1991.

Cross, Claire. *Church and People: England 1450–1660*. 2nd ed. Oxford: Blackwell, 1999.

Dickens, A. G. *The English Reformation*. 2nd ed. University Park: Pennsylvania State University Press, 1989.

Foxe, John. *The Acts and Monuments of John Foxe*. A new and complete edition, edited by Stephen Reed Cattley. 8 vols. London: Seeley & Burnside, 1837.

General Convention, *Journal of the General Convention of . . . The Episcopal Church, Philadelphia, 1997*. New York: General Convention, 1998, Resolution 1997-A080, 271–72.

Gilley, Sheridan, and W. J. Sheils, eds. *A History of Religion in Britain: Practice and Belief from Pre-Roman Times to the Present*. Oxford: Blackwell, 1994.

González, Justo L. *The Story of Christianity*. Vol. 2, *The Reformation to the Present Day*. San Francisco: Harper & Row, 1984.

Gough, Deborah Mathias. "The Colonial Church: Founding the Church, 1695–1775." In *This Far by Faith*. Edited by David R. Contosta. University Park: Pennsylvania University Press, 2012.

Hardwick, Charles. *A History of the Articles of Religion*. Philadelphia: Hooker, 1852.

Journal of the Proceedings of the Bishops, the Clergy and the Laity of the Protestant Episcopal Church in the United States of America: 1871. Potter & Co. (1872) 381.

Luther, Martin. *Luther's Works*. 82 vols. planned. St Louis: Concordia; Philadelphia: Fortress, 1955–1986; 2009–.

MacCulloch, Diarmaid. *Thomas Cranmer: A Life*. New Haven: Yale University Press, 1996.

Markham, Ian S. et al., eds. "The Lambeth Conference." In *Wiley-Blackwell Companion to the Anglican Communion*, 98. Chichester, UK: Wiley-Blackwell, 2013.

Miscellaneous Department. "The Life of John Wickliffe." Reprinted from an English Publication, *Washington Theological Repertory* 1.1 (September 1819) 42.

Mullin, Robert Bruce. *Episcopal Vision/American Reality: High Church Theology and Social through in Evangelical America*. New Haven: Yale University Press, 1986.

---

52. Anglican-Lutheran International Co-ordinating Committee, Communiqué, Hong Kong, 19–25 November 2014, Communiqué, http://www.anglicancommunion.org/media/102211/2014-ALICC-Communique-Final.pdf.

Prichard, Robert W. *A History of the Episcopal Church*. 3rd ed. New York: Morehouse, 2014.

Roberts, Dana L. *Converting Colonialism: Visions and Realities in Mission History: 1706–1914*. Grand Rapids: Eerdmans, 2008.

Schunka, Alexandra. "Mixed Matches and Inter-Confessional Dialogue: The Hanoverian Succession and the Protestant Dynasties of Europe in the Early Eighteenth Century." In *Mixed Matches: Transgressive Unions in Germany from the Reformation to the Enlightenment*. Editors David M. Luebke and Mary Lindemann, 139–44. New York: Berghahn, 2014.

Scott, Thomas. *The Articles of the Synod of Dort*. Philadelphia: Presbyterian Board of Publication, 1856.

Sykes, Norman. *The Church of England and Non-Episcopal Churches in the Sixteenth and Seventeenth Centuries: An Essay towards an Historical Interpretation of the Anglican Traditions from Whitgift to Wake*. London: SPCK, 1949.

———. *Daniel Ernst Jablonski and the Church of England: A Study of an Essay toward Protestant Union*. London: SPCK, 1950.

Thorndike, Herbert. "A Discourse of the Forbearance of the Penalties which a Due Reformation Requires." In *Works*. Oxford: Parker, 1854.

Sirota, Brent S. *The Christian Monitors: The Church of England and the Age of Benevolence*. New Haven: Yale University Press, 2014.

Williams, C. Peter. "British Religion and the Wider World: Mission and Empire, 1800–1940." In *A History of Religion in Britain: Practice and Belief from Pre-Roman Times to the Present*, edited by Sheridan Gilley and W. J. Sheils, 381–405. Oxford: Blackwell, 1994.

Woolverton, John Frederick. *Colonial Anglicanism in North America*. Detroit: Wayne State University Press, 1984.

3

Celebrating the Dynamic Legacy of the Reformation

An Indian Perspective

—J. Jayakiran Sebastian

Introduction

With the celebrations of the five hundredth anniversary of the Protestant reformation underway, the question regarding the impact of events that took place in a small German town five hundred years ago on lands and peoples far away takes on an urgent note. The American novelist, Philip Roth, writes: "People think of history in the long term, but history, in fact, is a very sudden thing."[1] This "sudden thing" has had enduring consequences in unimaginable ways. While this is not the place to offer an encapsulated history of Christianity in India and Asia[2], I want to focus on the coming of the first Protestant missionaries to India around three hundred and ten years ago, the celebrations of this event, including at the level of the Indian government, then focus on how this history has impacted the life of one individual (the writer of this essay) in multifarious ways, circle back to the first missionaries, and conclude with the recognition that

1. Roth, *American Pastoral*, 87.
2. One fine resource for this are the books by Moffett, *A History of Christianity in Asia, Volume I—Beginnings to 1500*, and *A History of Christianity in Asia, Volume II—1500–1900*.

the "sudden thing" has a significant, persistent, and lasting impact at the individual, local, national, and international levels.

Continuing to Encounter Ziegenbalg Today

The fruits and legacy of the Protestant Reformation were directly carried to India in and through the first Protestant missionary, Ziegenbalg, who arrived in south India in 1706.[3] Three hundred years later, in 2006, the Government of India issued a stamp to commemorate this event.[4] One has to revisit and wrestle with the life and legacy of Ziegenbalg in order to understand the various facets of the encounter between Christianity and the religions of India, a reality that still pervades Indian Christianity more than three hundred years after the arrival of Ziegenbalg in Tranquebar (or Tharangambadi, the local name of this small town). It is encouraging that much work has been going on in the last couple of years to unfold more and more dimensions of his contribution and to understand the man, his mission, and his impact.[5]

Within a very short time of coming to India, Ziegenbalg claimed to have mastered the language, and started to delve deep into Tamil literature, wrote grammatical works, investigated proverbs and cultural practices, organized meetings between the practitioners of the local religion which involved religious "disputation," started educational opportunities, and set up a printing press, among many other achievements. Much of this was done in the face of various forms of opposition, especially by the Danish colonial authorities in Tranquebar. This was despite the fact that Ziegenbalg held a direct appointment in his task from the King himself and that he, along with his fellow missionaries, "were directly accountable to the king, and not to any civil or ecclesiastical administrators and committees, not even to the local governing council of the colonies."[6]

---

3. See the fine work by Singh, *The First Protestant Missionary to India*. See J. Sebastian under the title: "A Child of His Times," in *The Book Review*, Vol. XXIV, No. 8 (August 2000), 11–12.

4. See http://www.istampgallery.com/bartholomaeus-ziegenbalg-india-stamp/

5. Most importantly by Daniel Jeyaraj in many solid and groundbreaking books, including *Bartholomäus Ziegenbalg*. Also see *A German Exploration of Indian Society* and his "Colonialism and Mission in Tranquebar" in Oommen and Hans Iversen, eds., *It Began in Copenhagen*, 101–24.

6. Jeyaraj, *A German Exploration of Indian Society*, 32.

Although Indian thinking in the field of interreligious encounter continues to flourish,[7] with the Indian experience playing a prominent role in several such writings, as for example by people like Raimundo Panikkar,[8] S. J. Samartha,[9] M. Thomas Thangaraj,[10] Paul Knitter,[11] and K. P. Aleaz,[12] a fresh look at Ziegenbalg's approach and attitude to the religions and society of South India will repay us through the shock of recognition that many attitudes and opinions that are bandied about today have their roots in the past.[13]

At this point, I want to pick out a few issues and themes from the Dedication to King Fredrick IV of Ziegenbalg's "Detailed Description of the South Indian Society" and offer them as examples to provoke further writing and research. For the context and an analysis of the contents I can only urge the readers to peruse the outstanding introductory and explanatory material by Jeyaraj, including a detailed manuscript analysis and an exploration of the peregrinations and vicissitudes of the manuscript version/s in Europe.

Since I want to focus on the Dedication, it is necessary to note that in classical antiquity, patristic literature and down to recent times, the practice of dedicating a book to a patron has been prevalent. Even at the risk of digressing, a parallel from the field of music is instructive. The great composer Johann Sebastian Bach (1685–1750) dedicated the shorter version of what would become the great *Mass in B Minor* to the new Elector Fredrick Augustus II in 1733 along with the following letter:

> To Your Royal Highness I submit in deepest devotion the present small work of that science which I have achieved in *musique*, with the most wholly submissive prayer that Your Highness will look upon it with Most Gracious Eyes, according to Your Highness's World-Famous Clemency and not according to the poor *composition*; and thus deign to take me under Your Most Mighty Protection. For some years and up to the present moment, I have had the

---

7. The most recent contribution being that of Muthuraj Swamy, *The Problem with Interreligious Dialogue*.

8. Among his voluminous writings see Panikkar, "The Jordan, the Tiber, and the Ganges," 89–116.

9. Most prominently, S. J. Samartha, *One Christ—Many Religions*.

10. Thangaraj, *The Crucified Guru*.

11. Knitter, "It's Working," 157–182, notes, 199–202.

12. Aleaz, "Pluralism Calls for Pluralistic Inclusivism" 162–75.

13. See J. Sebastian, "Intertwined Interaction," 162–77.

Directorium of the Music in the two principal churches in Leipzig, but have innocently had to suffer one injury or another, and on occasion also a diminution of the fees accruing to me in this office; but these injuries would disappear altogether if Your Royal Highness would grant me the favor of conferring upon me a title of Your Highness's Court Capelle, and would let Your High Command for the issuing of such a document go forth to the proper place. Such a gracious fulfillment of my most humble prayer will bind me to unending devotion, and I offer myself in most indebted obedience to show at all times upon Your Royal Highness's Most Gracious Desire, my untiring zeal in the composition of music for the church as well as for the orchestra, and to devote my entire forces to the service of Your Highness, remaining in unceasing fidelity Your Royal Highness's most humble and ardent servant.[14]

This plea certainly reflects the client-patron realities of those times in Western Europe. For Bach his time in Leipzig, with the unending demands on his time and talents (including the requirement to teach Latin to the choir-boys of St. Thomas School) was never easy, and in spite of the fact that the working conditions were very demanding, he produced some of his greatest works during this period. These include great organ works, oratorios like the St. Matthew's and the St. John's Passions, as well as the Mass in B Minor, the second part of the 48 Preludes and Fugues, the Goldberg Variations and the Art of the Fugue. With calm fortitude and courage, Bach faced the trivial jealousies and petty expectations of small-minded and utterly mediocre church administrators and bureaucrats. In addition to his duties at the various churches of Leipzig, and the need to provide for his growing family (a total of 20 children from his two marriages), Bach had to produce a new cantata for nearly every Sunday of the year, not to say anything of the extra demands of the various festivals of the Church year.[15] Given all this it is not surprising that he could appeal to the Ruler to at least provide him with a position that would give him a measure of financial stability, enclosing as it were, one of the gems of the Western classical musical tradition.

Given that the life spans of Ziegenbalg and Bach overlap, and given their importance in the history of Protestant Christianity, including in India, an examination of the Dedication of Ziegenbalg's work to King of Denmark is an interesting parallel, since what followed remains one of the

---

14. Quoted in Stapert, *My Only Comfort*, 43–44.
15. See Leisinger, *Bach in Leipzig*.

most significant sources of sociological and religious inquiry into the life of the peoples of South India at the beginning of the eighteenth century.[16]

After listing the titles of the King, the Dedication begins with the prayer that "God, the ruler of the heavens and the earth" would grant the king "a blessed government, and abiding joy of true blessing for body and soul in time as well as in eternity." Although Ziegenbalg did not go down the slippery slope of florid subservience in the prose which church historian of the fourth century Eusebius unblushingly employed,[17] nevertheless, the colonial characteristics of early Protestant Christianity, especially in terms of mission in terms of royal desire, and missionary research to fulfill occidental interest in things oriental, seen in the title page, where the book is described as presenting "in a comprehensive manner the theological as well as the philosophical principles and teaching of the South Indians that are based on their own writings and communicated to beloved Europe for useful learning"[18] was a typical feature which indicates the weight of the colonial baggage that characterized the encounter of Christianity with the peoples of the land. The patron had to be acknowledged, the patron had to be praised, and all efforts, in whatever direction, had to be oriented to the purposes of the patron, or if not oriented toward in the direct sense, at least shown to be important in fulfilling the purposes indirectly.

Following this, there is a listing of the manifold difficulties that the missionaries faced, including persecution, the wiles of Satan, and also "multiple obstacles" both in India and Europe. The formulaic language which talks about working and achieving something 'in spite of,' which no doubt reflects ground realities, also sets the missionary enterprise within

---

16. See In what follows, I am quoting from the Jeyaraj translation, in Jeyaraj, *Bartholomäus Ziegenbalg*, 60–61. For a comparable attempt in the 17th century, see the recent compilation and translation of three important works by Roberto de Nobili, including his "Report on Certain Customs of the Indian Nation."

17. The parallel is the famous oration by Eusebius in praise of the Roman emperor Constantine. The English translation is found in Wace, H and P. Schaff, *A Select Library of Nicene and Post-Nicene Fathers,* 581–610. This speech marks the point where it was openly acknowledged by the clergy of the church that the emperor was the deciding prime mover in the life and self-understanding, not to say anything about the theology, of the church. This in more than one sense marked the ascendancy of a ruler ideology in the life of the church. See Barnes, *Constantine and Eusebius* and Kee, *Constantine versus Christ.* Also, the outstanding article by Devin Singh, "Eusebius as Political Theologian," 129–54, compels us to reevaluate the evidence.

18. Jeyaraj, *Bartholomäus Ziegenbalg,* 59.

the framework of divine dispensation and heavenly teleology, a teleology of ultimate inevitable triumph.

Why then was this work undertaken? Ziegenbalg writes: "We intend to show in what kind of terrible [religious, spiritual] errors the South Indians live and how urgent it is to preach the Gospel of Jesus Christ for their salvation." This follows the methodological sequence which is found in much of the literature regarding why one ought to understand another group of people and their religious customs and practices, namely that in order to convert, one has to understand, in order to understand, one has to enter deep into the life and practices of the people; in order to correct, error must be understood, in order to triumph, evil should be detected and named. This is hardly the basis for inter-religious understanding, but is surely the basis of the desire to know and to name, in other words, the manifestation of the power of epistemology, epistemology understood from the point of view of the one doing the exploration and reporting.

What is it that the missionaries hoped to achieve? "All through our life we desire to heartily serve God and the Royal House of Denmark in an appropriate and useful manner so that through our present work many South Indians would be saved. These South Indian Christians will one day stand in front of the throne of God and thank Your Royal Majesty in all eternity for the grace and patronage given to the work, through which they are saved from their heathen blindness and converted to Christ, the Savior of the world." The rhetoric is quite clear—serving God and serving the Royal House of Denmark are telescoped into each other.[19] This has justifiably led to a deep rooted suspicion in the minds of certain commentators,[20] whose writings demonstrate a deeply held belief in the conspiracy theory of Christian missionary expansion, and the conviction that this continues to be the lodestar guiding even the sincere and well-meaning attempts at inter-religious understanding today. Such thinking feeds straight into the agenda of those who foster violence in the name of

---

19. See Sugirtharajah, *The Bible and Empire*, for an outstanding analysis of the "role" of the Bible in the imperial enterprise, and how it was "used" and "abused" by both the colonizer and the colonized. The companion volume to this is his *The Bible and the Third World*, 72–73, where Sugirtharajah points out that "Colonial interpretation makes it abundantly clear that hermeneutical issues are not settled by simply referring to texts alone. They are decided largely by the interpretative concerns of those who employ them."

20. Including Balagangadhara, *'The Heathen in His Blindness . . .'*

curbing conversions and are not at all prepared to recognize the complexity of the questions involved.[21]

The Dedication concludes with the predictable sentence assuring His Royal Majesty of prayer. This leaves no doubt at all as to where one's loyalty lay, a question that comes back to haunt Indian Christians today, when confronted with the question of the location of one's loyalty, geographical and personal.[22] One has to ask as to how and in what manner the 'body of knowledge' assembled by Ziegenbalg has left its residue in Indian Christianity and amongst Indian Christians today, especially in terms of 'embedded' attitudes towards the living religions of India.

It would be stretching things too far to lay the burden of the prospects and problems of inter-religious co-operation and understanding today on the ideas expressed in the Dedication written almost three hundred years ago. Yet, it seems to me, that while one ought to commend the incredibly painstaking task undertaken by Ziegenbalg in analyzing the society, customs, and mores of the people amongst whom he lived and worked, the intentionality should not be forgotten. It is not my purpose to point an accusing finger at Ziegenbalg. Rather we ought to use such occasions as the commemoration of the 300th anniversary of the Protestant presence in India to be introspective and ask ourselves as to how we, who have entered into this rich and varied legacy, have internalized, whether consciously or unconsciously, embedded attitudes to those who continue to live in accordance with their long-held faith practices. Reducing people to mono-identities and through "singular classification" based on presumed religious identity has been a bane of comparative religious studies, and Amartya Sen rightly and powerfully protests against this.[23] It is to the credit of Ziegenbalg that he glimpsed, albeit in a patronizing manner, the reality about goodness and truth being found amongst people of good will, wherever they come from and whatever their religious allegiances could be. In his work he writes:

> Even though the South Indian do not have the true scripture . . .
> of the Word of God, their conscience has convinced them that

---

21. See J. Sebastian, "Conversion and its Discontents," 165–72.

22. David Ludden notes: "Orientalism as a body of knowledge is today not only embedded in a vast corpus of official wisdom, scholarship, social theory, and empirical data. It is also embedded rhetorically and institutionally in political culture . . ." In his "Orientalist Empiricism," 272–73.

23. Sen, *Identity and Violence*.

they should avoid sinning, and do good things. They do this . . . to establish their self-righteousness. But if they would do this through faith in Christ Jesus, from the power of salvation that he has accomplished and also as a token of their gratitude to him, then they would have a splendid reward. And what they do can be considered good works. As they are now living in unbelief, one can say what the Holy Scripture expresses about such works. At the same time, we as Christians can notice how far the South Indians have progressed according to the natural light in their natural power. They invariably put us to shame because, though we have the teachings of faith in Christ Jesus, we remain unproductive.[24]

Why was it important to revisit this story and analyze it? Even as we rejoice and continue celebrating the life and legacy of Ziegenbalg, and even as we discover on Facebook a page devoted to the Ziegenbalg Museum Tharangambadi,[25] celebrations should be tinged with introspection and an ongoing desire, as those impacted by colonialism and the Protestant missionary expansion, to explore and examine these realities and not treat them as passé. Examples of this abound in terms of the ongoing discussions about the impact of bilateral, multilateral and ecumenical discussions on the unity of the church;[26] on how profoundly important ecumenical documents like the Baptism, Eucharist, and Ministry convergence agreement coming from the Faith and Order Commission of the World Council of Churches[27] have impacted the life of the church;[28] Christians and the nationalist movement[29]; how the emergence of Dalit theology continues to interrogate taken-for-granted "certainties," including the question of who interprets and writes history and theology;[30] and how the "inheritors" of the Reformation legacy theologize in their own contexts.[31]

24. Jeyaraj, *A German Exploration of Indian Society*, 130.

25. https://www.facebook.com/ziegenbalg.

26. One example is Thomas, *Conciliar Ecumenism*. The acronyms stand for the Church of South India, the Church of North India, and the Mar Thoma Church which have full communion agreements and are trying to move further ahead into a visibly more united church.

27. *Baptism, Eucharist and Ministry*, 111.

28. See the essay by the Indian Orthodox theologian, Kurien, "From 'anamnesis' to 'metanoia,'" 267–75.

29. One example which covers the geographical region first impacted by the early Protestant missionaries is D. Jeyakumar, *Christians and the National Movement*.

30. See the range of essays in Clarke, in *Dalit Theology in the Twenty-first Century*.

31. See J. Sebastian, "Contributions of Indian Christian Theology," 43–61.

Let me now personalize this and reflect on what these events have meant to me and how it has impacted my life.

Hybridized, Intertwined Identity: A Personal Note

Each human person embodies many facets, including the reality that we are all made of stardust.[32] At the same time, the journeys, influences, and experiences that have brought us to where we are and made us who we are, are distinctive and unique. Can one really offer a 'full disclosure'? I'm an ordained minister of the united Church of South India,[33] with deep family roots in the coming to India in 1834 of missionaries from the Basel Mission (who themselves, depending on whether they came from South Germany or North Switzerland, were Lutheran or Reformed[34]). My church belonging has been shaped by my home congregation, St. Mark's Cathedral in Bangalore, built in 1808 as an Anglican church which became the cathedral of the undivided Mysore Diocese of the Church of South India in 1947 and later of the Karnataka Central Diocese.[35] My theological thinking has been shaped by my having studied at the United Theological College in Bangalore[36] (itself a pioneer of inter-denominational, ecumenical theological education since 1910, founded because of the vision of a galaxy of eminent church leaders to start an interdenominational institution to offer high quality theological education so that leaders with a broader outlook and a deeper commitment to ecumenism could be produced for the churches in India, and supported in the early period by the London Missionary Society, the American Arcot Mission, the United Free Church of Scotland Mission, the American Board of Commissioners for Foreign Missions, and the Wesleyan Methodist Missionary Society). My education was furthered through other theological teachers, especially all my Dalit congregation members in my first parish—five village congregations formerly belonging

---

32. See http://www.physicscentral.com/explore/poster-stardust.cfm, accessed on January 8th, 2016.

33. See Oommen, "Challenging Identity and Crossing Borders," 60–67, for the antecedents, along with a discussion on ongoing challenges within the church.

34. The latest publication that addresses the background, as well as contemporary issues and themes, is Christ–von Wedel, *The Basel Mission*.

35. For an overview of the Diocese, see the book by its former bishop, Gill, *Roots to Fruits: Karnataka*.

36. See my dictionary entry, J. Sebastian, "United Theological College, Bangalore," 710–11.

to the congregational London Missionary Society.[37] Subsequently I served an urban congregation formerly belonging to the Wesleyan Methodist Mission, and, as a theological educator at the United Theological College in Bangalore, helping as an honorary associate presbyter in various congregations including a former Scottish Kirk. My formal theological training also comprises of having done my master's at the Orthodox Theological Seminary in Kottayam, Kerala[38] (founded in 1815 as the first Orthodox school of theology in Asia, an initiative supported by Colonel John Munroe, the British Resident in the kingdom of Travancore, because the seminary leadership had, at the beginning, a cordial and strong link with the Church Missionary Society missionaries who had just come to the state of Kerala). After spending almost two decades at the United Theological College, I now find myself teaching at the Lutheran Theological Seminary in Philadelphia, a seminary of the Evangelical Lutheran Church in America.[39] These are undoubtedly some of the facets that have shaped me, and to complicate matters just a little more, I'm the son of a Hindu convert who loved the organ music of J. S. Bach (but that's a story for another time, including two of my names, Johann and Sebastian!) The reality is that I'm someone encapsulating within my personal, ecclesiastical and ministerial identity the cosmopolitan hybridity, diversity, promise and potential of the shaking of the foundations set in motion by the Protestant reformation; influenced by the great movements toward the unity of the church in the twentieth century; and now part of the worldwide discernment of the future of theological education[40] within the messy complexities of life within the United States as the twenty-first century rumbles onwards.

Interactive Journeys and Enriching Encounters

To continue on a personal level—I relished being in Lutherstadt Wittenberg for a conference in August 2012 and I enjoyed my stay in the Leucorea, the University founded in 1502, where early on Luther was called to

---

37. I have reflected on my experiences in this context in several pieces of writing, including "Jud(as)signing Blame," 98–103; "On Walking Through the Cemetery," 178–189; and "Evoking the Bible at a Funeral in an Indian-Christian Community," 124–30.

38. 2015 marks the bicentenary of this venerable institution (http://www.ots.edu.in/).

39. For some of the background and analysis, see Trexler, *High Expectations*.

40. See J. Sebastian, "Engaging Multiculturalism as Public Theologians," 335–43, where I build upon my work both in Bangalore and Philadelphia to address this issue.

be a Professor, followed later by Melanchthon. It had enough time to visit the Luther house and see every exhibit and read every descriptive plaque, and also to admire the magnificent new display on how daily life in the Luther household was run by Katharina von Bora, his wife, with audio and visual components, including the sounds of water being drawn from the well and ducks being slaughtered. I was disappointed to see the Melanchthon Haus swaddled in construction tarps, but read about how the new exhibition that would open there would focus on this great figure and his role in university reforms world-wide. The opportunity to worship in the City Church and soak in the great altar piece of Cranach the Elder, with its evocative representation of the sacraments and the centrality of the Word, was meaningful at multiple levels, as was worshiping in the Castle Church and contemplating the stark simplicity of the graves of Luther and Melanchthon, flanked by the statues of prominent figures from the time of the Protestant reformation.

It was good to use this opportunity to remember Wilhelm Kling, a German Lutheran missionary from the Evangelische Landeskirche in Württemberg, a mechanic who came out to India in 1928 and served at the Mission Station of Puttur, a small town, then 10 hours from Mangalore by bullock-cart and ferry.[41] Mangalore was where the pioneer missionaries from the Basel Mission, mainly coming from South Germany and North Switzerland, began their mission work in 1834.[42] This was an opportunity to recall Annaiah Pujary, a priest of the Bhuta or spirit cult of the toddy-tapping community, who responded to the preaching of the early missionaries and became one of the early converts, along with his family, and in whose direct line on the maternal side I come from. Many years later Rev Kling must have been surprised to find a panic-stricken woman carrying a small baby begging for refuge after having fled her village, where her husband had been killed in a land-dispute by members of the family, who in fear of her life and that of her small child, ran through the forest with no possessions to the one place where she knew help could be had. In due course she was baptized "Ruth" and the baby "David," my father. His first memory is that of the funeral of the little child of the Klings, and how all the children in the orphanage followed the casket to the cemetery. In 1986, on a

41. An evocative photograph of Puttur and the Klings is found at http://digitallibrary.usc.edu/cdm/singleitem/collection/p15799coll123/id/24774/rec/10, part of the stunning International Missionary Photography Archive, accessed on January 8th, 2016.

42. See Norman Sargant, *From Missions to Church in Karnataka*, 129–169, for details.

visit to Puttur, my wife Mrinalini's, hometown, I rediscovered the damaged and almost unrecognizable grave of baby Kling. At that time I was far from Wittenberg, but in another sense I had come home, and the rediscovery of my father's childhood memory connected me with another place and another time in more senses than one.

Thinking back to my time in Wittenberg it was amusing to walk out of the Leucorea and look for a place to have something to eat, and almost bang opposite find what I thought was a Turkish Imbiss, where I used my German to order a Doner Kebab, only to find the puzzled owner asking me in Hindi (which I don't know too well) whether I wouldn't rather have an Indian biryani instead! Yes—there is not only a Maharani Restaurant in Wittenberg, but also a Taj Mahal restaurant very close to where another great Reformer, Johannes Bugenhagen, had been buried. These Indians are everywhere—and here you can blame the reformation for that!

Yes—the message of the Bible and the legacy of the Reformation that began in Germany has travelled far and wide and the hope of salvation in and through Jesus has touched the hearts and lives of many people all over the world. Of course things were happening years, decades, and centuries before the events in the early 16th century in Wittenberg, but the reformation provided impulses and proved to be a catalyst impacting people, places, events, and epochs in ways that the great reformers in Germany, Switzerland, the Netherlands, and beyond could never have imagined.[43]

Events engender consequences—Luther knew that, and despite what awaited him offered up for debate the Ninety-Five theses, the ninety-fourth of which states that Christians should follow Christ at all cost.[44] The consequences of discipleship, especially in terms of the world-wide missionary movement, and the reality that events in the little German town of Wittenberg; events amidst the dusty roads of Galilee; events in the small town of Puttur in India; events taking place where I now work, at the Lutheran Theological Seminary at Philadelphia, are all ongoing testimony to the liberating and loving power of our Lord, drawing together people across places, across space and time, overcoming possible limitations with the limitless possibilities of the promise that "if the Son makes us free, we shall be free indeed" (John 8:36).

43. See J. Sebastian, "Interrogating Christian Practices," 255–66.

44. A fresh translation into English by Timothy Wengert, with an elaborate introduction, is found in Wengert, ed., *The Annotated Luther*, 13–46. Article 94 is translated: "Christians must be encouraged diligently to follow Christ, their head, through penalties, death, and hell . . . " (46).

We now return to the Reformation legacy and examine how local contexts and congregations continue to grapple with the lasting significance of this, even as the dizzying pace of life hurtles onwards in 21st century India.

Inheriting the Reformation Legacy in Another Land, Another Time—Reformed Realities

"The sand around Lake Geneva" has been used as a negative metaphor in a footnote of an important article on the legacy of the *Baptism, Eucharist and Ministry* document after twenty-five years.[45] However, the sand around the lake which witnessed many dramatic moments in the life of the church, not just during the tumultuous years of the reformation in the sixteenth century, but also in the second half of the twentieth and early twenty-first centuries, has dissipated in various ways and in a variety of forms and settled down, only to be stirred up again in countries far from the land of their origin. While the transformation and transference of water has been used as a metaphor in many pieces of theological writing, I have not seen too many instances of the use of sand. The great Indian Nobel-Prize winning writer, Rabindranath Tagore, in his poem "Where the Mind is Without Fear" spoke of the "dreary desert sand of dead habit." He was hoping that reason would not flounder there, but in recent years the rediscovery of silica, or to give it its chemical name silicon dioxide, in the high-tech hardware computer industry has brought back renewed attention to sand as something that is so abundant and readily available, and is in fact the most abundant mineral on the surface of the earth and this has raised its 'profile' immensely! Sand, although inert, carries with it echoes and memories, and the sand around Lake Geneva has carried more than its fair share of such echoes and memories to distant places around the world.

Memories of the sand offer us an occasion to recall and recollect those who in the midst of the sixteenth century were prepared to stand up for the power of their convictions, and in this process, set in motion the ongoing reformation of the church, reminding us that we cannot take anything for granted, but must constantly return to the springs of the water of life, emerging from the sand, returning to the scriptures and the

---

45. See note 44 on p. 23 of the article by Geoffrey Wainwright, "Any Advance on 'BEM'?" 1–29, where he talks about how the study on the apostolic faith, following the publication of *Confessing the One Faith* (1991), "unfortunately ran into the sand around Lake Geneva."

message of Jesus, recognizing that our faith is not something sterile, but something living, not something arid, but something active, not something dull, but something dynamic, not something to be taken lightly, but something that continues to enliven and revive the church today. Among such people are Martin Luther, Huldrich Zwingli, and Jean Calvin whose lives, writings, witness and testimony, continue to illumine the life of our churches in ways that they never dreamt of, and in countries that they had never heard of, today.

As we reflect on these great forebears of our faith-journey, we need to remember and recollect that they based their convictions on the power of the Biblical testimony, and constantly returned to the refreshing sources of life to be found in the Bible. For them, the reading, listening, hearing, and interpretation of the Bible, under the power of the Spirit, was the font of renewing and rekindling the faith. They tried to embody in their lives the commitment to the ideal that "all who exalt themselves will be humbled, and all who humble themselves will be exalted" (Matthew 23:12).

The 16th century Protestant Reformation and our commemoration of the values of the reformation remind us of several ideals that we have to continue to inculcate in the life of the church, wherever we live, work, or worship, today:

- at a time when more and more people are moving away from reading and rediscovering the world of faith testified to in the Bible, and depending on self-proclaimed prophets and interpreters of the Bible, most of whom are interested in promoting themselves, their families, or their organizations, the reformation principle regarding the centrality of the Bible in the life of every person, and the affirmation that the Bible is there to be read and understood, and is not a cult object to be idolized, has to be underlined. As Calvin noted in his Preface to the Commentary on the Psalms: "It is by perusing these inspired compositions that [we] will be most effectively awakened to a sense of [our] maladies, and, at the same time, instructed in seeking remedies for their cure."[46]

- the assertion that we are members of a mixed body of wheat and weeds and are simultaneously both saints and sinners has to be understood in the present-day context, where crassly consumerist "blessing ideology" has trivialized the understanding of sin, where corruption

---

46. Translated in Thornton, *Calvin, Steward of God's Covenant*, 165.

is condoned, where the cult of the powerful is fostered, where hero-worship of those in positions of power and authority is growing. We have to recognize ourselves for what we are—those who "however unworthy we may be to experience His help, nevertheless for love of His name He holds out His hand to us, He calls us to Himself"[47]—those who to whom God offers the gift of forgiveness, through the self-offering of Jesus; the gift of unconditional love and the promise of unmerited grace through the life and death, resurrection and ascension of Jesus

- the reminder of the centrality of God in a world of consumerism has to be underscored. Especially at a time when economic uncertainty and fear regarding our long term economic future are at a peak, concern for the poor which was never a major priority is in danger of being ignored altogether under the excuse that the present economic scenario leaves all of us vulnerable to market forces which were lauded when times were good, but leave us bewildered and looking for quick and easy ways of pinning the blame on vulnerable scapegoats when times are difficult. How can the church continue to offer to all kinds of people, especially those facing the downside of a rapacious-consumerist and acquisition-oriented ideology gone crazy, signs of hope, peace and reconciliation?[48]

One Example and Several Questions

For four years, in the 2000's, I served in an honorary capacity as the Associate Presbyter of St. Andrew's Church of the Karnataka Central Diocese of the Church of South India. This venerable old church, which became part of the united church was originally founded more than 150 years ago as the St. Andrew's Kirk, serving the Scottish expatriate community, especially those in various military regiments and working for organizations like the Indian Railways during the colonial period, and later, after

---

47. Calvin's sermon—exposition on Psalm 115:1–3, translated and edited by McKee in the section "Weekday Worship in Calvin's Geneva," 171.

48. See J. Sebastian,"Having and Sharing: Theological Perspectives, 112–126. The prominent American novelist and essayist, Marilynne Robinson calls for the rediscovery of "Calvinistic wonder" even while recognizing the complexity and paradoxical nature of his life and legacy in her "Preface to the Vintage Spiritual Classics Edition" of Thornton, *John Calvin: Steward of God's Covenant*, ix–xxvii.

the independence of India, those who had stayed on in various capacities. There was an earlier connection to this church, and that was through the fact that I was a classmate of the son of the last Scottish Presbyter of this church, Rev. Robert W. Rentoul, and have fond memories of playing in the compound and in the parsonage, still called the 'Manse,' in the early 60's. For some time my father helped as the organist of this church, and I recall him practising on the pipe organ with an organ blower manfully pumping away at the bellows in the days before the electric motor to run the instrument was installed. I can see in my mind's eye the plain long altar table in front of the stained glass window, with the grave of an important member of the congregation just behind it, and the words of the commandments engraved on the wall admonishing me. I remember a wall plaque in memory of a member who was "eaten by a tiger," and also recollect drawing aside a curtain behind the side altar to reveal a beautifully carved white marble statue of a reclining woman.

More than fifty years after these vivid memories, the church continues to be maintained very well with major renovation projects completed on the pipe organ and on repainting the church after propping up the weakened foundations of the bell tower. The busy traffic of Bangalore continues to whiz by on the roads in front and behind, and frenzied construction activity is visible all around, but the church continues to be home to a lively and growing congregation, served by a series of pastors, including one who went on to become the Bishop of the Diocese, and then the Moderator of the Church of South India, Rt. Rev. S. Vasanthakumar.

Legacies have value when they are not forgotten and continue to endure, but at the same time, do not become reified to such an extent that they become idealized. India has now been independent for almost seventy years, and the sleepy city of Bangalore has become a huge metropolis, the hub of the world's software industry, whose seams have already burst with the influx of people not only from all over India, but from different corners of the world. St. Andrew's Church has not been immune to these changes and this is reflected in the changing character of the congregation. There are certainly those who long for an imagined past and are nostalgic for times gone by, but others want to look ahead and seek ways and means of continuing to be a church in tune with the times and catering to the needs and expectations of people living in a city in transition.

It's interesting that the plain wooden altar displays signs of what I have referred to in a sermon as "creeping Anglicanisation" in terms of becoming more elaborately "decorated" with the silk tablecloth, vases of flowers, the cross in the middle and lamps around. The step separating the choir from the nave is now used as the place where people gather and kneel in rows to receive the eucharist, and new altar rails have been installed. It's instructive that people seem to be unaware of a pattern of worship in an old Scottish Kirk, where the method of the distribution of elements happened in a way, with communicants distributing elements among themselves once it had been passed on, that would now seem rather unusual to them. I find it curious and yet offer the observation that while there is so much pride taken in maintaining the building and joy in preserving the heritage of the past, when it comes to the line of sombre-looking Scottish clergymen displayed in fading photographs in the vestry, there is not much awareness in who they were, their names, and no real interest in filling the "gaps" in this record.

In another land, at another time, such observations raise important questions when it comes to understanding the reformed legacy.[49] The example of St. Andrew's Church reveals that the vitality of this tradition within the united Church of South India has undergone a momentous transformation and is revivified under rubrics and categories which display a sense of continuity with the past, but under the practicalities of having brought a variety of confessional standpoints together under one umbrella, allowed for the blossoming of an enriched understanding of what it means to be a living church in a minority situation.

Reflecting on the legacy of the Basel Mission in India, on the occasion of the celebration marking 150 years of the arrival of this mission in India, Stanley Samartha asked the following pointed questions:

> the question is much more than just a matter of names, or labels or ethnic identity. It is indeed a matter of spiritual legacy which is important. The question then would be this. How can those components in our legacy which we hold to be precious be preserved in order that they might make a contribution to the larger stream of life in the Church of Christ in India? Conversely, the Church of Christ in India should also ask itself how the legacies of different streams that have joined it . . . be made to feel that their identities

---

49. For an outstanding range of essays addressing this, see the two volumes, Alston, *Reformed Theology: Identity and Ecumenicity* and *Reformed Theology: Identity and Ecumenicity II—Biblical Interpretation in the Reformed Tradition*. The Indian Biblical scholar, D. R. Sadananda, has an important chapter in the second volume: "The Johannine Logos: Interpreting Jesus in a Multi-Religious Context," 349–72.

are not being submerged and that their legacies not swallowed up, but recognised as contributing to the spiritual growth and maturity of the Church of Christ in India?[50]

The legacy of a particular tradition endures in a variety of forms and values including the ongoing importance given to an active worship life, not confined to the church but spilling over to a commitment to the transformation of life in society; the deep desire to uphold the rich traditions of Biblically-based preaching and teaching, and discern insights from the Biblical witness in the vastly changed terrain of the country, where in spite of modernization, the incredible growth of the entrepreneurial class, and the persistence of degrading poverty, modern India continues to have "a way of confounding you and still making you laugh about it."[51] Obviously one cannot laugh when confronted with degrading and dehumanizing poverty, and the persistence of intolerant fundamentalism is undoubtedly a worrying phenomenon. Separating insinuations from reality, and simplistic attribution of motives from a more nuanced understanding of issues is a pressing task.[52] Thus, the reformed legacy includes the openness and willingness to dialogue with the context, something that contributes to the vigour of church life in India.[53] In this sense, as was pointed out regarding a different context, where the ideological standpoints of the Reformation seemed to clash and even contradict one another, "[i]n their differently formulated but common rejections of the twin ethical errors of casuistic legalism and situational license, Luther and Calvin, along with Melanchthon and Martin

---

50. Samartha, "Digging Up Old Wells," 85–95, here, 91.

51. Part of the conclusion of Luce, *In Spite of the Gods,* 356. Also see Khanna, *Billions of Entrepreneurs.* For a more sober assessment of the reality of life in India, see Ramachandra Guha, *India After Gandhi.*

52. For example, writing from the perspective of the "tribal" communities of North-East India, specifically from the state of Mizoram and from within the tradition of the Welsh Presbyterian church, Rosiamliana Tochhawng has examined and interrogated the "Ten Articles of Faith" of the Presbyterian Church of India, and notes that

[a] critical and constructive study of a theological tradition held on by the church also aims to make a significant contribution to the construction of a relevant contextual theology. Explication of a theology in its historical context would indicate its historical limitation and consequently allow new voices in the context to speak through the official theological standards of the church.

In Tochhawng, *A Study of the Ten Articles of Faith,* 5.

53. See the timely and pertinent analysis of Swamy, *The Problem with Interreligious Dialogue.*

Bucer, do all finally unite together in endorsing a biblical ethic of norms based on a theology of grace."[54]

Living out life in church and society, a life welcoming the renewal of life brought about by the bubbling springs of water that emerge from the sand, whether the pebbles around Lake Geneva, or the gravel surrounding St. Andrew's Church in Bangalore, the reformed legacy within the animated life of the church in India has proved to have enduring worth, even though the sands have been shifted and displaced, inhabiting other territories, only to be stimulated and stirred up again, offering the ongoing possibility of new ways of faithfulness emerging out of the sand, to invigorate the inheritance of the reformation even in this our twenty-first century.

Particularity Encountering Reality: Another Example of Doctrinal Documents and Throbbing Life

Examples can be multiplied, but let me offer just one example of what happens when doctrinal texts encounter realities of life by turning again to the cusp of the great Protestant missionary expansion of the church at the beginning of the eighteenth century. I find it intriguing that just when the first Protestant missionaries to India, Bartholomaeus Ziegenbalg and Heinrich Plutschau were getting ready to be commissioned to go out as missionaries in the Danish colony of Tranquebar in South India, there was a rediscovery of the twenty-eighth article of the Augsburg Confession. This article, depending on which version and which draft one uses has the title "Concerning the Power of Bishops" and "Concerning the Church's Power."[55] It talks about the power of bishops and the power of the church in juxtaposition with the secular power or the power of the sword. Can these powers be mixed? The argument is that this cannot be the case and that "everyone should honor and esteem with all reverence both authorities and powers as the two highest gifts of God on earth." In other words "the powers of the church and civil government must not be mixed." What has all this to do with India, or for the matter, with the world today?

Article 17 ("Concerning the Return of Christ to/for Judgment"[56]) regarding a secular kingdom, could be interpreted in terms of the rejection of

---

54. Part of the conclusion of Lazareth, *Christians in Society,* 244–45.

55. See the translations of both the Latin and German versions of "Article 28 of the Augsburg Confession."

56. Ibid., 50–51.

millennial secular kingdom teaching, leading to a particular understanding of the role of the Lutheran rulers and princes for those who lived in their territories, namely the duty of fostering the true evangelical faith amongst their subjects, something that did not apply to those "outside" this authority. This could mean that "it simply made no sense to go out and do missionary work among the heathen outside the prince's realms and countries."[57]

Article 28 goes on to talk about bishops not having the power to establish anything contrary to the gospel. It reiterates that "the chief article of the gospel must be maintained, that we obtain the grace of God through faith in Christ without our merit and do not earn it through service of God instituted by human beings." The point in all this, as argued by some theologians at that time, was that this presupposed the existence of a congregation, an assembly where regulations could be made "for the sake of love and peace." How does all this apply to a situation, especially in the context into which early missionaries where heading, where there was no congregation, where a community has not been called and gathered around the preaching of the gospel and the administration of the sacraments?

The Bishop of Zealand, Henrik Bornemann, when confronted by the request of the court chaplain to the King of Denmark to ordain two German students from the University of Halle, embodied this dilemma and managed to block the ordination by failing them in the candidacy process by questioning their orthodoxy on grounds that they were pietists. When the bishop was confronted by King Fredrik IV and the Queen, a reexamination was held, this time in the residence of the Court Chaplain, and this time there was a different understanding of the sacred and the secular, as well as of the heathen subjects of the kingdom in that far-off toe-hold of Denmark in India, Tranquebar, and the two students passed the examination and were ordained, and six days later received their commission to be royal missionaries to the East Indies. It was emphasized that the two must adhere to the right teachings and teach the "poor blind heathen" who live in that area (a trading colony of Denmark in India) and within its borders. The task entrusted to these missionaries was to "hold and handle there in Eastern India nothing besides the holy doctrine as it is written in God's Word and repeated in the Symbolic Books of this realm after the Augsburg Confession, and teach nothing besides it."[58] Were the European universi-

---

57. See Glebe-Møller, "The Realm of Grace Presupposes the Realm of Power," 156–77.

58. The translation "Royal Appointment and Instructions to the First Missionaries,"

ties and mission agencies prepared for what would be a flood of Malabar "heathen" and "pagan" religious literature that Ziegenbalg, within a short period would collect, translate, and transmit to Europe?[59] The challenge then was to understand how the exquisite religious literature in Tamil could be read "according to the Augsburg Confession."

There is much that we can learn and much that we can unlearn from the attitudes and behavior of pioneers like Ziegenbalg.[60] Although hermeneutical lenses and methods of interpretation are always in flux, and that which was seen to be an unquestionable given at a particular point in time is now being interrogated from a postcolonial perspective, one can continue to read and resignify issues in the fecund interplay between gospel and cultures in another time and in a different context.

I hope that our postcolonial suspicion will not be superseded or subsumed, but contribute to shaping, creatively and profitably, the dialogical imagination that is so much in danger of being lost in a world of monovalent analysis, swamped as we are by the ever-present reality of violence and terrorism,[61] and recognize that even when it does not appear to be the case, there was always room for the "other" in the always generous and every ready church, especially for the vulnerable, and those from Dalit and Tribal backgrounds in India, who found in the message of the Gospel the power of the powerless and the assurance of welcome.[62]

New situations call forth new responses and new ways of faithfulness. Rowan Williams reminds us that we need to talk about "the *true* relationships of which existing systems are a distorted reflection."[63] Given the real-

---

is found in Gross, *Halle and the Beginning of Protestant Christianity in India*, 1337–39.

59. In an interconnected world, it is incumbent on us to take the conclusion of a major book on the legacy of what happened in the middle of the last millennium seriously: "Awareness of the Reformations' contributions to the development of our world both helps us understand how we got that way and provides a critical horizon for evaluation of the results," in Lindberg, *The European Reformations*, 378.

60. See Rajan, "Cultural Delimitations," 1221–39.

61. See the range of contributions in Janes, *Martyrdom and Terrorism*. Also see Salisbury, *The Blood of Martyrs* for a careful analysis of how the texts and events of the past impact upon the anxieties and frustrations of the present.

62. For Tribal responses, see, among others, Pachuau, *Ethnic Identity and Christianity*; Lalpekhlua, *Contextual Christology*; Longchar, *Returning to Mother Earth*; and Basumatary, *Ethnicity and Tribal Theology*. For Dalit realities, histories and responses, see, among others, Webster, *The Dalit Christians*, and Jeremiah, *Community and Worldview among Paraiyars of South India*.

63. Williams, *On Christian Theology*, 229.

ity of how existing systems, especially of global and structural inequality function in contemporary society, we need to recall, recognize, and reconceptualize another time, another place, another way of believing, another way of being in the world, and what the "contact zones" and global interconnections meant and mean.[64]

And, finally, having traversed paths that have taken us near and far, paths that have led us into ways of being and believing that seem rather distant from the hopes of the early reformers, paths on which we have been accompanied and helped by those with whom we may have very little in common, including the practices of a life of faith, paths on which we met disciples who name other names and claim other allegiances, paths where the journeys of faith will continue[65], we look for where the way, Christ, will lead us, recognizing that he is the sure foundation, a foundation on which we can continue to thrive and face every challenge, confident that the vicissitudes of the present and the dire predictions of the future will not prevail and that the path will truly be for us the goal.[66]

Bibliography

Aleaz, K. P. "Pluralism Calls for Pluralistic Inclusivism: An Indian Christian Experience." In *The Myth of Religious Superiority: A Multifaith Exploration*, edited by Paul F. Knitter, 162–75. Faith Meets Faith Series. Maryknoll, NY: Orbis, 2005.

Alston, Wallace M. Jr., and Michael Welker, eds. *Reformed Theology: Identity and Ecumenicity*. Grand Rapids: Eerdmans, 2003.

Alston, Wallace M., and Michael Welker, eds. *Reformed Theology: Identity and Ecumenicity II—Biblical Interpretation in the Reformed Tradition* Grand Rapids: Eerdmans, 2007.

Balagangadhara, S. N. *The Heathen in His Blindness . . . : Asia, the West and the Dynamic of Religion*. Studies in the History of Religion 64. Leiden: Brill, 1994.

Baptism, Eucharist and Ministry. Faith and Order Paper 111. Geneva: World Council of Churches, 1982.

Basumatary, Songram. *Ethnicity and Tribal Theology: Problems and Prospects for Peaceful Co-existence in Northeast India*. Oxford: Lang, 2014.

---

64. On this I have been privileged to learn from Mrinalini Sebastian, especially her recent articles: "Basel Mission in South West India," 176–202, nn. 26–268; and "Localized Cosmopolitanism and Globalized Faith," 47–64.

65. This would include ongoing questions on how the liturgy continues to enliven the church, on which see Kumar, "Liturgical Reforms," 247–61, and the newly revised, *The Church of South India*.

66. Sections of this essay depend upon some of my articles, including "'God and the Royal House of Denmark,'" 35–41; "'. . . not hurrying on to a receding future, nor hankering after an imagined past': Edinburgh 1910, T. S. Eliot, Postcolonial Missiology, and Our Mission to God," 79–92; "The Always Generous and Every Ready Church," 139–48.

Christ-von Wedel, Christine and Thomas K. Kuhn, eds. *The Basel Mission: People, History, Perspectives 1815–2015.* Basel: Schwabe, 2015.

Clarke, Sathianathan. *Dalit Theology in the Twenty-first Century: Discordant Voices, Discerning Pathways,* edited by Deenabandhu Manchala and Philip Vinod Peacock. New Delhi: Oxford University Press, 2010.

Gill, Kenneth. *Roots to Fruits: Karnataka Central Diocese—Record of the First Thirty Years.* Bangalore: Asian Trading Corporation, 2001.

Glebe-Møller, Jens. "The Realm of Grace Presupposes the Realm of Power: The Danish Debate about the Theological Legitimacy of Mission to the Heathen." In *It Began in Copenhagen: Junctions in 300 years of Indian-Danish Relations in Christian Mission,* edited by George Oommen and Hans Raun Iversen, 156–77. Delhi: ISPCK, 2005.

Gross, Andreas, Y. Vincent Kumaradoss, and Heike Liebau, eds. "Royal Appointment and Instructions to the First Missionaries. In *Halle and the Beginning of Protestant Christianity in India: Vol. III: Communication between India and Europe.* Halle: Franckeschen Stiftungen zu Halle, 2006. 1337–39.

Guha, Ramachandra. *India after Gandhi: The History of the World's Largest Democracy.* Delhi: Picador, 2007.

Janes, Dominic and Alex Houen. *Martyrdom and Terrorism: Pre-Modern to Contemporary Perspectives.* Oxford: Oxford University Press, 2014.

Jeremiah, Anderson H. M. *Community and Worldview among Paraiyars of South India: 'Lived' Religion.* London: Bloomsbury, 2013.

Jeyakumar, D. Arthur. *Christians and the National Movement: The Memoranda of 1919 and the National Movement with Special Reference to Protestant Christians in Tamil Nadu: 1919–1939.* Bangalore: Centre for Contemporary Christianity, 2009.

Jeyaraj, Daniel. *Bartholomäus Ziegenbalg: The Father of Modern Protestant Mission—An Indian Assessment.* Delhi: ISPCK, 2006.

———. *A German Exploration of Indian Society: Ziegenbalg's 'Malabarian Heathenism.'* Chennai: The Mylapore Institute for Indigenous Studies, New Delhi: ISPCK, 2006.

———. "Colonialism and Mission in Tranquebar—Their Relationship to the 'Hindus.'" In *It Began in Copenhagen: Junctions in 300 Years of Indian-Danish Relations in Christian Mission,* edited by George Oommen and Hans Raun Iversen, 101–24. Delhi: ISPCK, 2004.

Khanna, Tarum. *Billions of Entrepreneurs: How India and China are Reshaping their Futures and Yours.* Boston: Harvard Business School Press, 2007.

Knitter, Paul F. "It's Working: Examples of a Globally Responsible Dialogue." In *One Earth Many Religions: Multifaith Dialogue and Global Responsibility,* 157–82. Maryknoll, NY: Orbis, 1995.

Kolb, Robert, and Timothy J. Wengert, eds. "Article 28 of the Augsburg Confession." In *The Book of Concord: The Confessions of the Evangelical Lutheran Church.* Minneapolis: Fortress, 2000.

Kumar, Santosh S. "Liturgical Reforms: A Review of the Church of South India Eucharistic Liturgy." *Studia Liturgica* 44.1–2 (2014) 247–61.

Kurien, Jacob. "From *'anamnesis'* to *'metanoia'*—Beyond Convergence Texts, Towards Attitudinal Conversion." In *BEM at 25: Critical Insights into a Continuing Legacy,* edited by Thomas F. Best and Tamara Grdzelidze, 267–75. Geneva: WCC Publications, 2007.

Lalpekhlua, L. H. *Contextual Christology: A Tribal Perspective.* Delhi: ISPCK, 2007.

Lazareth, William H. *Christians in Society: Luther, the Bible, and Social Ethics*. Minneapolis: Fortress, 2001.

Leisinger, Ulrich. *Bach in Leipzig*. Translated by Victor Dewsbery. Berlin: Edition Leipzig, 2000.

Lindberg, Carter. *The European Reformations*. 2nd ed. Chichester, UK: Wiley Blackwell, 2010.

Longchar, A. Wati. *Returning to Mother Earth: Theology, Christian Witness and Theological Education—An Indigenous Perspective*. Tainan: Programme for Theology and Cultures in Asia. Kolkata: SCEPTRE, 2012.

Ludden, David. "Orientalist Empiricism: Transformations of Colonial Knowledg." In *Orientalism and the Postcolonial Predicament: Perspectives on South Asia*, edited by Carol A. Breckenridge and Peter van der Veer, 272–73. Philadelphia: University of Pennsylvania Press, 1993.

Luce, Edward. *In Spite of the Gods: The Rise of Modern India*. New York: Anchor, 2007,

McKee, Elsie Anne, ed. and trans. "Weekday Worship in Calvin's Geneva." In *John Calvin, Writings on Pastoral Piety*. Classics of Western Spirituality. Mahwah, NJ: Paulist, 2001.

Moffett. Samuel Hugh. *A History of Christianity in Asia*. 2 vols. Maryknoll, NY: Orbis, 1992–2005.

Oommen, George." Challenging Identity and Crossing Borders: Unity in the Church of South India." *Word and Worship* 25.1 (2005) 60–67.

Pachuau, Lalsangkima. *Ethnic Identity and Christianity: A Socio-Historical and Missiological Study of Christianity in Northeast India with Special Reference to Mizoram*. Studies in the Intercultural History of Christianity 129. Frankfurt: Lang, 2002.

Panikkar, Raimundo. "The Jordan, the Tiber, and the Ganges." In *The Myth of Christian Uniqueness: Toward a Pluralist Theology of Religions*, edited by John Hick, and Paul F. Knitter, 89–116. Faith Meets Faith Series. Maryknoll, NY: Orbis, 1987.

Roth, Philip. *American Pastoral*. New York: Houghton Mifflin, 1997.

Salisbury, Joyce E. *The Blood of Martyrs: Unintended Consequences of Ancient Violence*. New York: Routledge, 2004.

Samartha, Stanley J. "Digging Up Old Wells: Reflections on the Legacy of the Basel Mission in India." In Godwin Shiri, ed., *Wholeness in Christ: The Legacy of the Basel Mission in India*. Mangalore: Karnataka Theological Research Institute, 1985.

———. *One Christ—Many Religions: Toward a Revised Christology*. Maryknoll, NY: Orbis, 1991. 3rd Indian ed. Bangalore: South Asia Theological Research Institute, 2000.

Sargant, Norman. *From Missions to Church in Karnataka, 1920–1950*. Madras: Christian Literature Society, 1987.

Sebastian, J. Jayakiran. "The Always Generous and Every Ready Church." In *Communion on the Move: Towards a Relevant Theological Education—Essays in Honour of Bishop John Sadananda*, edited by Wati Longchar and P. Mohan Larbeer, 139–48. Bangalore: BTESSC, 2015.

———. "Conversion and its Discontents." *Bangalore Theological Forum* 32 (2000) 165–72.

———. "Evoking the Bible at a Funeral in an Indian-Christian Community." *Asia Journal of Theology* 26 (2012) 124–30.

———. "Having and Sharing: Theological Perspectives from India on Consumerism and Exclusion." *International Journal of Public Theology* 1 (2007) 112–26.

———. "Interrogating Christian Practices: Popular Religiosity Across the Ocean." In *Baptism Today: Understanding, Practice, Ecumenical Implications*, edited by Thomas F. Best. Faith and Order Paper 207. Collegeville, MN: Liturgical, 2008.

———. "Intertwined Interaction: Reading Gregory of Nazianzus Amidst Inter-religious Realities in India." In *A World for All? Global Civil Society in Political Theory and Trinitarian Theology*, edited by William F. Storrar, et al., 162–77. Grand Rapids: Eerdmans, 2011.

———. "Contributions of Indian Christian Theology towards the Ongoing Theologizing in the Indian Context." In *Christian Theology: Indian Conversations—Volume I: Dogmatic Themes*, edited by Samuel George and P. Mohan Larbeer, 43–61. Bangalore: BTESSC, 2016.

———. "Engaging Multiculturalism as Public Theologians." *International Journal of Public Theology* 8 (2014) 335–43.

———. "God and the Royal House of Denmark'": "Continuing to Encounter Ziegenbalg Today." *Gurukul Journal of Theological Studies* (Special Issue on "The Life and Ministry of Bartholomaus Ziegenbalg") 17.2 (July 2006) 35–41.

———. "Jud(as)signing Blame." In *Still at the Margins: Biblical Scholarship Fifteen Years after the 'Voices from the Margin,'* edited by R. S. Sugirtharajah, 98–103. London: T. & T. Clark, 2008.

———. "'. . . not hurrying on to a receding future, nor hankering after an imagined past': Edinburgh 1910, T. S. Eliot, Postcolonial Missiology, and Our Mission to God." *Bangalore Theological Forum* 46 (2014) 79–92.

———. "On Walking Through the Cemetery: Continuity and Transformation in Reading Death in an Indian-Christian Community." In. *Postcolonial Interventions: Essays in Honor of R. S. Sugirtharajah*, edited by Tat-siong Benny Liew, 178–89. Bible in the Modern World 23. Sheffield: Sheffield Phoenix, 2009.

———. "United Theological College, Bangalore." In *The Oxford Encyclopaedia of South Asian Christianity* 2:710–11. New Delhi: Oxford University Press, 2012.

Sebastian, Mrinalini. "Basel Mission in South West India" Language, Identity, and Knowledge in Flux," In *Cultural Conversions: Unexpected Consequences of Christian Missionary Encounters in the Middle East, Africa, and South Asia*, edited by Heather J. Sharkey, 176–202. Syracuse: University of Syracuse Press, 2013.

———. "Localized Cosmopolitanism and Globalized Faith: Echoes of 'Native' Voices in 18th and 19th Century Missionary Documents." In *European Missions in Contact Zones: Transformation through Interaction in a (Post-)Colonial World*, edited by Judith Becker, 47–64. Veröffentlichungen des Instituts für Europäische Geschichte Mainz, Abteilung für Abendländische Religionsgeschichte. Supplement 107. Göttingen: Vandenhoeck & Ruprecht, 2015.

Singh, Brijraj. *The First Protestant Missionary to India: Bartholomaeus Ziegenbalg (1683–1719)*. Delhi: Oxford University Press, 1999.

Stapert, Calvin R. *My Only Comfort: Death, Deliverance, and Discipleship in the Music of Bach*. Grand Rapids: Eerdmans, 2000.

Sugirtharajah, R. S. *The Bible and Empire: Postcolonial Explorations*. Cambridge: Cambridge University Press, 2005.

Swamy, Muthuraj. *The Problem with Interreligious Dialogue: Plurality, Conflict and Elitism in Hindu-Christian-Muslim Relations*. Bloomsbury Advances in Religious Studies. London: Bloomsbury Academic, 2016.

Thangaraj, M. Thomas. *The Crucified Guru: An Experiment in Cross-Cultural Christology.* Nashville: Abingdon, 1994.

Thomas, V. V. *Conciliar Ecumenism: The Beginning of the Former CSI-CNI-MTC Joint Council.* Bangalore: BTESSC/SATHRI, 2008.

Thornton, John F., and Susan B. Varenne, eds. *John Calvin, Steward of God's Covenant: Selected Writings.* New York: Vintage, 2006.

Tochhawng, Rosiamliana. *A Study of the Ten Articles of Faith of the Presbyterian Church of India.* Delhi: ISPCK, 2007.

Trexler, Edgar R. *High Expectations: Understanding the ELCA's Early Years, 1988–2002.* Minneapolis: Augsburg Fortress, 2003.

Wainwright, Geoffrey. "Any Advance on 'BEM'? The Lima Text at Twenty-Five." *Studia Liturgica* 37.1 (2007) 1–29.

Webster, John C. B. *The Dalit Christians.* Rev. ed. Delhi: ISPCK, 2009.

Wengert, Timothy J., ed. *The Annotated Luther: Vol. I—The Roots of Reform.* Minneapolis: Fortress, 2015.

Williams, Rowan. *On Christian Theology.* Challenges in Contemporary Theology. Oxford: Blackwell, 2000.

4

The Five-Hundredth Anniversary of the Reformation

A Catholic Perspective

—Jacob W. Wood

Inasmuch as Reformed and Catholic theologians engaged one another with reasoned arguments, a similarly pressing question for all sides of the controversies of the sixteenth century was to what extent the Fathers of the Church—and in particular, Augustine—could be claimed in support of one another's views. The chief difficulty for Western theologians at the time was trying to find a balance across Augustine's teaching on the necessity of grace, his teaching on the freedom of the will, and his teaching on the unity of the Church. It was not an easy task, as each one of these doctrines was formed amidst a different controversy—Augustine's teaching on the necessity of grace against the Pelagians, his teaching on the freedom of the will against the Manichees, and his teaching on the unity of the Church against the Donatists—indeed, it is not always clear that Augustine himself had in fact, or had intended to work them out into a fully coherent dogmatic system. So much have subsequent theologians struggled with the task of that integration that historiographies of the Reformation over the course of the last half-century have been colored by a narrative which tends to polarize one aspect of Augustine's thought against another. Thus the well-known summary of B.B. Warfield, recognized—albeit critically—by Alistair McGrath, pits Augustine's teaching on the necessity of grace against his teaching on the unity of the Church: "[I]t is Augustine who gave us the Reformation. For the Reformation, inwardly considered, was just the ultimate triumph of Augustine's doctrine of grace over Augustine's doctrine of the Church."[1]

Yet as is often the case, history eludes such simplification. More recent scholarship on the period surrounding the Reformation has pointed out the vast variety of Augustinianisms that took shape.[2] It would be more accurate to say that all sides of the Reformation struggled in nuanced ways to integrate the themes inherited from the Bishop of Hippo, and that given the magnitude and complexity of his thought—to say nothing of the magnitude and complexity of the various "Augustinianisms" to which it gave rise—differences of interpretation abounded.

It would be beyond the scope of this essay to attempt an historical exegesis of Augustine that reduced or reconciled those differences. The purpose of this essay is rather to describe, albeit briefly, the history of attempts in the last 500 years within the Catholic Church to integrate the three aforementioned Augustinian themes: the freedom of the will, the necessity of grace, and the unity of the church. Marking out five significant dates along the way, I will suggest that the ascendency of Suarezian Congruism in debates about free will and grace after the Council of Trent led to a vision of the unity of the Church focused on the pope as the sole absolute monarch on earth, a vision which in turn raised questions about the relationship between unity and freedom. Although Vatican I seemed to canonize the Suarezian system, its failure to describe completely the relationship between the pope and the rest of the Church left open the opportunity for Vatican II to re-envision that relationship as a relationship as a communion, grounded in the unity of the persons of the Trinity, and freely entered into by grace. This renewed self-understanding opened the Catholic Church to ecumenical dialogue in the decades that followed, and can serve as a basis from which to pursue the goal of complete ecumenical unity today.

---

1. Warfield, *Calvin and Augustine*, 322.
2. See, for example, Saak, *Creating Augustine*.

The Tridentine Decree on Justification (January 13, 1547)

The trajectory of post-Reformation Catholic Augustinianism was determined by the Decree on Justification issued at the sixth session of the Council of Trent on January 13, 1547. In its fifth chapter, the decree upheld both the necessity of grace and the freedom of the will. If we are to be *justified*, it is necessary that grace move us towards justification; if it is *we* who are to be justified, it is necessary that our own free will move us towards justification as well.[3] In this double affirmation, the Decree took its lead from the Augustinian synthesis of the medieval theologian, Thomas Aquinas, who in its wake was declared a Doctor of the Church:

> God ... moves all things according to the mode of each ... Wherefore he also moves human persons towards justice according to the condition of human nature. But a human person has the power of free choice from his own nature. And therefore ... a motion from God towards justice does not occur without a motion of free choice; rather, God so infuses the gift of justifying grace that he moves our free choice simultaneously with it to accept the gift of grace.[4]

The Tridentine Decree also proscribed two views on justification from the Catholic Church, which the Council Fathers thought misrepresented the relationship between grace and the free will: that Christ's merits are

---

3. Council of Trent, Decretum de iustificatione, in Decrees of the Ecumenical Councils, ed., Tanner, 2 vol., 2:672. "Declarat [Concilium] praeterea, ipsius iustificationis exordium in adultis a Dei per Christum Iesum praeveniente gratia sumendum esse, hoc est, ab eius vocatione, qua ullis eorum existentibus meritis vocantur, ut qui per peccata a Deo aversi erant, per eius excitantem atque adiuvantem gratiam ad convertendum se ad suam ipsorum iustificaitonem, eidem gratiae libere assentiendo et cooperando, disponantur, ita ut tangente Deo cor hominis per Spiritus sancti illuminationem neque homo ipse nihil omnino agat, inspirationem illam recipiens, quippe qui illam et abiicere potest, neque tamen sine gratia Dei movere se ad iustitiam coram illo libera sua voluntate possit. Unde in sacris litteris cum dicitur: *Convertimini ad me, et ego convertar ad vos*, libertatis nostrae admonemur; cum respondemus: *Coverte nos Domine ad te, et convertemur*, Dei nos gratia praeveniri confitemur."

4. Aquinas, *S.T.*, 1-2.113.3.co., in Opera Omnia, vol. 7, 332. "Deus ... movet omnia secundum modum uniuscuiusque ... Unde homines ad iustitiam movet secundum conditionem humanae naturae. Homo autem secundum propriam naturam habet quod sit liberi arbitrii. Et ideo ... non fit motio a Deo ad iustitiam absque motu liberi arbitrii; sed ita infundit donum gratiae iustificantis, quod etiam simul cum hoc movet liberum arbitrium ad donum gratiae acceptandum ..."

the sole formal cause of justification and are extrinsically attributed to the sinner by means of a forensic declaration, or that it is necessary for such a forensic declaration to supplement an interior, formal sanctification in the just.[5] To the minds of the Council Fathers, both views suffered from the difficulty that they held up one Augustinian theme (the necessity of grace) to the expense of the other (the freedom of the will, as healed by grace).

The purpose of the Tridentine decree was not to dispel all debate within the Catholic Church as to the nature of justification, although it did certainly establish narrower boundaries for that debate than had existed previously. Nor was its purpose to solve every theological problem connected with the proclamation that grace moves the will, but freely. Quite the reverse: the Tridentine decree challenged Catholic theologians in the Post-Reformation period not only to affirm the freedom of the will, but also to explain *how* it could be reconciled with the necessity of grace.[6] That reconciliation was a mystery that no theologian—including Aquinas—had hitherto been able to explain completely.

Vive la différence! The End of the *De auxiliis* Controversy (March 19, 1607)

Following the Council of Trent, two principal schools of thought emerged among Catholic theologians on the question of how grace relates to the free will. The first of these flourished among the theologians of the Society of Jesus (the Jesuits), and was inspired by Luis de Molina, S.J. (1535–1600).[7] The second school of thought flourished among the theologians of the Order of Preachers (the Dominicans), and was inspired by Domingo Báñez, O.P. (1528–1604).[8]

---

5. The former was understood as Luther's understanding of justification; the latter as the so-called "double justice" theory advocated by Girolamo Seripando at the Council. Luther's rejection was intentional. See M Luther, *De servo arbitrio*, English translation: *On the Bondage of the Will*, trans. J. I. Packer. Seripando did not reject the freedom of the will explicitly and intentionally, but such a rejection was taken to be logically implied by his thought: he affirmed the need for an extrinsic imputation of the merits of Christ even after the inward formation of the heart by charity; to the Council Fathers, he thereby implicitly denied the sufficiency of that charity to cause a free and just will For a summary of the discussions at Trent surrounding the double justice theory, see Malloy, *Engrafted into Christ*, 59–122; Rondet, *Gratia Christi*, 273–76.

6. McGrath, *Iustitia Dei*, 90.

7. For an introduction to Molina's life and works, see MacGregor, *Luis de Molina*.

8. There does not exist an introduction in English to Báñez as there does to Molina.

In 1588, Molina published a work called the *Concordia*, in which he sought to show how the freedom of the human will could be reconciled with God's grace.[9] He defined freedom in terms of indifference: "we call an agent free who, given everything required for action, can either act or not act, or can so perform one action that he can also perform its opposite."[10] In more technical language, Molina explained that God, as the first cause, gives human persons, as secondary causes, everything needed to act by means of a "general concurrence."[11] That is the "everything required for action," to which his definition refers. It is up to the human person to take that power in hand and determine it to a specific action.[12]

Molina's definition of freedom easily explained the freedom of the will. Molina himself described the relationship between God and the free will like two people pulling one boat: neither is the cause of the boat's motion without the other; each contributes a part.[13] It also easily explained how, although God is the first cause of movement in creatures, God has no participation in human sin: the determination of the will towards a specific, sinful action, is completely up to the human person who chooses to so determine his or her will.[14] But Molina's thought was also subject to two difficulties. The first of these concerned the doctrine of Providence: how can God be said to be Provident over actions which are completely at the whim of human freedom? The second of these concerned the necessity of grace: how can grace be said to be necessary for the act of justification if all specific human actions, including those involved in justification, proceed directly from a created will?

Molina explained Providence by means of God's foreknowledge. God, he says, has three kinds of knowledge: natural, free, and middle

---

Instead, see Cuadrado, *Domingo Báñez (1528–1604)*.

9. Luis de Molina, *Concordia liberi arbitrii cum gratiae donis*, A second, revised edition was released in 1595. Partial English translation: *On Divine Foreknowledge: Part IV of the "Concordia* (Ithaca: Cornell, 1988). Reference will be made to the first Latin edition.

10. Luis de Molina, *Concordia liberi.*, q. 14, a. 13, disp. 2 [Ribeiro 12]. "illud agens liberum dicitur quod positis omnibus requisitis ad agendum potest agere et non agere aut ita agere unum ut contrarium etiam agere possit."

11. Ibid., disp. 28 [Ribeiro 182].

12. Ibid., disp. 28 [Ribeiro 182].

13. Ibid., disp. 27 [Ribeiro 174].

14. Ibid., disp. 31 [Ribeiro 194].

knowledge.[15] Natural knowledge is the knowledge whereby God knows all universals (e.g. "human nature"); it is logically prior to God's choice to do anything in particular about the things he knows. Free knowledge is that whereby God knows all of his particular decisions (e.g. "I will create such and such an individual person with a human nature"); it entails God's choice to act on his knowledge and it is logically posterior to natural knowledge. In between these two, Molina argues, stands "middle knowledge" (*scientia media*), whereby God foreknows the truths of future contingents ("if I were to create such and such a person with a human nature, he or she would make such and such specific choices"). Like natural knowledge, middle knowledge does not involve God's choice to do anything in particular—*ipso facto* it does not impose any necessity on the potential contingents known by it; like free knowledge, middle knowledge concerns concrete individual choices and events.[16] God's Providence over free creatures takes place particularly in virtue of middle knowledge. God foreknows what all individual people will do without forcing them to do it.[17]

Molina's understanding of grace is based on his understanding of middle knowledge. God, as 1 Timothy 2:4 says, wills that all men be saved. No one, however, can be saved without grace. Molina interprets this Scripture to mean that God has a real will for the salvation of all, that God offers grace to all.[18] However, we can say logically that, prior to God's choice to offer grace to a given individual, he foreknows by his middle knowledge that were he to offer grace to the elect, they would accept it; were he to offer it to the reprobate, they would reject it. In actual fact, when he chooses with his free will to offer grace, the elect accept it, while the reprobate reject it. Everything happens according to God's middle knowledge, but God's middle knowledge does not compel it to happen.[19]

Báñez thought that Molina compromised the sovereignty of God and the necessity of grace. He returned to Molina's image of two people pulling a boat. Each moves the ship with its own power, and neither has any direct influence over the other. This gives creatures a radical independence from God which neither reason nor Scripture can support.[20] The problem, as

15. For what follows, see ibid., disp. 50 [Ribeiro 329].
16. Ibid., [Ribeiro 330].
17. Ibid., [Ribeiro 333–35].
18. Ibid., disp. 38 [Ribeiro 229].
19. Ibid., disp. 38 [Ribeiro 332]; see also McGrath, *Iustitia Dei*, 94.
20. Domingo Báñez, *De vera et legitima Concordia liberi arbitrii create cum auxiliis*

Báñez saw it, lay in Molina's understanding of the concurrence which God gives to created wills. Báñez thought that a general concurrence was insufficient; without a *specific* concurrence, determining the will to a *specific* act, no created will would be able to choose anything whatsoever.[21] Báñez described this specific concurrence as a "physical pre-motion." Since no creature would move were it not sustained in being and given motion by God,[22] in order for a person to perform any act, it is necessary that they receive a prior motion (hence "pre-motion") from God, impelling their will to act.[23] This pre-motion operates in the manner of an efficient cause, impelling the will towards a specific choice (hence, a "physical" pre-motion), rather than a final cause, enticing it to act (a "moral" pre-motion).

Báñez's understanding of the free will had the opposite difficulties of Molina's: it struggled in explaining the freedom of the will and sin, although it had an easier time explaining the necessity of grace. As concerns the free will, saying that God gives an efficacious premotion towards a specific action seems to imply a deterministic compulsion towards that action. Báñez was aware of this objection. He excused himself from the objection by appealing to the distinction between necessity in the one acting (*necessitas consequentis*) and necessity of the action taking place (*necessitas consequentiae*). God, as the first cause of all motion in nature, acts in accord with the natures he has made. God acts "sweetly" (*suaviter*) (Wisdom 8:1); he always brings about the effects he intends, but he does so without taking control of the things that bring those effects about.[24] With regard to sin, Báñez distances God from participation from sin by means of the same distinction between physical causes and moral causes with which he described premotion in the first place. While God is the *physical* cause of the will's act (otherwise there would be no act at all), God is not the *moral* cause of the will's choosing to perform a given act sinfully. God impels the

---

gratiae Dei efficaciter moventis humanam voluntatem 2.1.4, in *Comentarios inéditos a la Prima Secundae de Santo Tomás*, 3:376.

21. Domingo Báñez, *Scholastica Commentaria in Primam Partem Summa Theologicae S. Thomae Aquinatis*, q. 14, a. 13, 362. "si concursus primae causae non esset efficax ad determinandum omnes causas secundas, nulla secunda causa operaretur suum effectum: quia nulla secunda causa potest operari, nisi sit efficaciter a prima determinata."

22. Báñez, *De vera et legitima Concordia* 2.1.5, in *Comentarios inéditos*, 3:378.

23. Domingo Báñez, *De vitiis et peccatis*, 1–2.79.4.48, in *Comentarios inéditos*, 2:229.

24. Báñez, *Scholastica Commentaria in Primam Partem*, q. 19, a. 8, 427.

will to an action which he foreknows a person will perform as a sin; but God never forces, entices, or encourages the person to choose it *as a sin*.[25]

As Molina's general concurrence influenced his understanding of grace, so Báñez's specific concurrence influenced his understanding of grace. Báñez begins with the observation that, while Christ's sacrifice was sufficient for the salvation of all, that sacrifice does not have its proper effect in all: some people are lost entirely; others receive the grace they need to reach the heights of sanctity, and that grace does not achieve its full effect in them.[26] He adds to this the presupposition, established previously, that whatsoever God wills to cause in a creature infallibly takes place in that creature.[27] He concludes that God does not give the same grace to all, as Molina had supposed. There is an *intrinsic* difference between sufficient grace, which is objectively enough but fails to bring about its intended effect, and efficacious grace, which actually brings about its intended effect.[28] The universal salvific will referred to in 1 Timothy 2:4 should not be taken as indicating that God offers the same grace to all persons *absolutely speaking*; if it did, all persons would be saved. To the contrary, " . . . simply speaking, God does not want every person to be saved."[29] The universal salvific will is something that God causes in human beings rather than something which exists really in God; since the human intellect can consider an act without all its attendant circumstances, God causes the saints to desire the salvation of every person, that is, until they consider the justice of God towards sinners, and the mercy of God shown to the just in the punishment of sinners, which reminds the just of how serious their own sins were.[30]

From 1597 to 1607, the Holy See attempted to come to a determination as to whether Molinism or Bañezianism was the correct way to describe how grace and the free will relate to one another. It did this in the context of the *Congregatio de auxiliis*, a series of 85 meetings sponsored by the Holy See, including dozens during which theologians from both sides disputed for as many as seven hours on end.[31] Ultimately, the two positions

---

25. Báñez, *De vitiis et peccatis*, 1-2.79.4.22, in *Comentarios inéditos*, 2:211.

26. Báñez, *De vera et legitima Concordia* 2.3.6, in *Comentarios inéditos*, 3:392.

27. Ibid., *De vera et legitima Concordia* 2.3.6.

28 Báñez, *Comentarios inéditos*, 3:393.

29. Báñez, *De vera et legitima Concordia*. 2.4.7, in *Comentarios inéditos*, 3:406. "simpliciter loquendo [Deus] non vult omnem hominem salvum fieri."

30. Ibid., 2.4.7.

31. Hardon, *History and Theology of Grace*, 258; McGrath, *Iustitia Dei*, 94; Rondet,

were argued to a standstill. On September 5, 1607, Pope Paul V decided that enough was enough; he ended the sessions and forbade that "in treating this question anyone criticize the side [of the debate] opposite his own, or assign it any sort of censure," and further entreated the two sides, "to abstain from very harsh words, which signify bitterness of heart."[32] The Pope indicated that he would consider the matter further and issue a decision at the appropriate time.

The promised decision never came, and so all sides were—and still are—permitted to hold their differing views about the relationship between free will and grace.[33] Bañezianism survived the *De auxiliis* controversy relatively unscathed. Molinism survived mainly in a modified form known as Congruism, and proposed by the theologian, Francisco Suárez, S.J. (1548–1617).[34] Suárez followed Molina's understanding of the radical freedom of the will and on the nature of God's middle knowledge, but supplemented it with Báñez's emphasis on the radical priority of grace and consequent distinction between sufficient and efficacious grace: God specifically decrees which individual persons are to be saved. Respecting their freedom to accept or reject grace, he offers them grace which he foreknows that they will accept by his middle knowledge precisely "*because* he foresees it will be efficacious."[35]

Gratia Christi, 294–306.

32. DH 1997. "In negotio de auxiliis facta est potestas a Summo Pontifice cum disputantibus tum consultoribus redeundi in patrias aut domus suas: additumque est, fore, ut Sua Sanctitas declarationem et determinationem, quae exspectabatur, opportune promulgaret. Verum ab eodem Ss. Domino serio admodum vetitum est, in quaestione hac pertractanda ne quis partem suae oppositam aut qualificaret aut censura quapiam notaret . . . Quin optat etiam, ut verbis asperioribus amaritiem animi significantibus invicem abstineant."

33. For subsequent papal declarations reaffirming the "non-condemnation," see Hardon, *History and Theology of Grace*, 259–61.

34. For an introduction to the life and works of Suárez, see Salas, "Introduction," 1–28.

35. Hardon, *History and Theology of Grace*, cited in Salas, "Introduction," 14 (emphasis in original). For the primary source, see Suárez, *De gratia* 5.21.4, in *Opera Omnia*, 8:498. " . . . Vocatio efficax illa est quae de facto habitura est infallibiliter effectum a vocante intentum, et ideo, licet in se sit gratia praeveniens a solo Deo facta, nihilominus includit habitudinem ad cooperationem futuram liberi arbitrii, cum auxilio gratiae simultaneo, et consequenter includit quamdam congruitatem respectu personae cui datur, ut sit illi ita proportionata et accommodata, sicut oportet, ut in tali persona, in tali tempore et occasione infallibiliter effectum habeat, et per hoc habet illa vocatio quod congrua et efficax sit." See Rondet, *Gratia Christi*, 299–301.

Gallicanism and Church Unity: *The Declaration of the Clergy of France* (March 19, 1682)

To say that Bañezianism and Congruism remained acceptable alternatives for Catholic theologians after the conclusion of the *De auxiliis* controversy is not to say that they were equally influential. Congruism had a significantly larger impact on the Catholic Church in view of the way in which it could be used to describe the relationship between the State and the Church. For, when James I of England published his *Premonition* of 1608,[36] reasserting the divine right of kings and criticizing the interference of the pope in temporal matters,[37] Suárez critiqued James's understanding of political government because he thought it subverted on a political level the freedom which Suárez had defended in the *De auxiliis* controversy on a philosophical and theological level.

In his treatise, *Defense of the Catholic Faith against the Errors of the Anglican Sect*,[38] Suárez agreed with James that God is the bestower of monarchical power. But where James sees monarchy as a power given by God *directly* to the king *over* those subject to him and, and hence the king is not accountable to his subjects,[39] Suárez sees monarchy as a power given by God *indirectly* to the king *through* those subject to him. Recalling Aristotle's observation in the *Politics* that human society originates when people come together naturally out of mutual need and for mutual assistance,[40] Suárez adds that political community arises from an exercise of the freedom inherent in the persons who make up that community. Anticipating in a germ form the social contract theory which would gain traction later in the seventeenth century, Suárez explains that while God has bestowed political authority directly upon human beings, God has bestowed that authority on the *entire community* of human beings, not on any one individual.[41] Humanity exists, as it were, in a natural state of democracy, unless or until a given human community freely decides to transfer some of its democratic power to a few of its members, in which case it becomes an aristocracy, or

---

36. James I, *A Premonition to All most Mightie Monarchies*, 110–68.

37. For a more systematic presentation of the ideas presented in the *Premonition*, see James I, *The Trew Law of Free Monarchies*, 53–70.

38. Suárez, *Defensio Fidei Catholicae adverus Anglicanae Sectae Errores*.

39. See James I, *Premonition*, 153–54.

40. Aristotle, *Politics, The Basic Works of Aristotle*, 1.2 (1252, a24–1253, a39).

41. Suárez, *Defensio fidei Catholicae* 3.2.3; 3.2.5, in *Opera Omnia* 24:206–7.

to one of its members, in which case it becomes a monarchy.⁴² There can be a variety of forms of government, including a variety of forms of monarchy, depending on how, to what extent, and under what conditions a given people has freely transferred its democratic power to some more limited number of people among them.⁴³

To say that human communities have an inherent freedom is not to say, however, that they are created radically independent of Christ and the Church. Suárez goes on to explain that, inasmuch as human community proceeds from human nature, it is only ordered towards the ends which human nature can achieve of its own accord without the assistance of grace: temporal happiness and temporal peace. But just as God directs human persons to a higher, supernatural end, which they cannot achieve without grace, so likewise God directs human communities to a higher, supernatural end, which they cannot achieve without grace.⁴⁴ In the Church, human community is raised up into a divine community, a "spiritual republic,"⁴⁵ which is " . . . no less . . . one kingdom in its order than is any temporal kingdom in its order."⁴⁶ Like a human society, the Church has a monarch, Christ, who governed the Church *per se* when he walked this earth; now that he has ascended into heaven, he governs the Church vicariously through his vicar, the pope.⁴⁷ This means that, alone of all monarchs on the earth, the Pope is the only one possessing a monarchy *directly* from God and who is not accountable to those under him; all other monarchs possess their monarchy *indirectly*, mediated through the consent of their people. Temporal rulers may have the right to exercise supreme power in temporal

---

42. Ibid., 3.2.7, 3.2.9, in *Opera Omnia*, 24:208–9.

43. Ibid., 3.2.4, in *Opera Omnia*, 24:207.

44. Ibid, 3.5.2, in *Opera Omnia*, 24:224–25.

45. Ibid., 3.6.2, in *Opera Omnia*, 24:231.

46. Ibid., 3.6.10, in *Opera Omnia*, 24:234. "Ecclesia Christi universa non minus est una, seu regnum unum in suo ordine, quam sit regnum quodlibet temporale in suo." Suárez's fellow-Jesuit, Robert Bellarmine, famously summarized this understanding of the Church: "The Church is a group of people just as visible and palpable as is a group of Roman people, or the kingdom of France, or the Republic of Venice." Compare Bellarmine *De controversiis christianae fidei*, 3.2, in *Opera Omnia*, 2:75. "Ecclesia enim est coetus hominum ita visibilis et palpabilis, ut est coetus populi Romani, vel regnum Galliae, aut respublica Venetorum."

47. Suárez, *Defensio*, 3.6.8 in *Opera Omnia*, 24:233. See Costigan, *The Consensus of the Church*, 22–31.

matters, but they have an indirect duty to order that civil life towards the divine life mediated to humanity through the Church.[48]

By and large, Dominican theologians did not put up any significant opposition to Suárez's opinions about the State and the Church, because the Bañezian understanding of free will and grace lent itself to a similar ideal of a human society elevated and perfected in the unity of the Church under the pope. In fact, Dominican theologians, and in particular Bartolomé de las Casas, O.P. (d. 1566) were particular champions of the freedom of native peoples.[49] However, an alternative to Congruism's understanding of free will and grace came to the fore at this time, which challenged both Jesuit and Dominican understandings of the Church. That alternative came to bear the name of "Augustinianism," not because of any more or less objective faithfulness to the Bishop of Hippo—nearly all Catholic theologians at this time were attempting to find a way of harmonizing the three Augustinian themes of the freedom of the will, the necessity of grace, and the unity of the Church—but rather because its adherents claimed Augustine as their patron, and cited him foremost as the source of their doctrine.

One of the first Augustinians of the Post-Reformation period was Michel de Bay (commonly known by the Latin, Michael Baius; 1513–1589).[50] Unlike Suárez, who clearly distinguished the unaided and natural use of our free will from the supernatural use of our free will under the influence of grace, Baius denied that grace supernaturalizes the will at all. He thought that when God made Adam and Eve, God's plan was to raise them to the beatific vision if they did good works with their unaided free will.[51] Consequently, Baius thought that the Fall was not the loss of a gratuitous gift so much as the spoiling of human nature; it wounded the human will such that we no longer possess the freedom to do good works.[52] Even in a state of

---

48. Suárez, *Defensio*, 3.5.6 in *Opera Omnia*, 24:226.

49. For the life of Las Casas, see Clayton, *Bartolomé de las Casas*.

50. For an overview of Baius and the Baianist controversy, see Donnelly, "Baius and Baianism," in *The New Catholic Encyclopedia*, 2:19; Rondet, *Gratia Christi*, 287–93; Simmonds, "Jansenism: An Early Ressourcement Movement?" in *Ressourcement*, 25. On its impact within Catholic theology, see de Lubac, *Augustinianism and Modern Theology*, 1–30.

51. Baius, *De meritis operum* 1.4, in *Opuscula Theologica*, 8, cited. in Rondet, *Gratia Christi*, 288.

52. Ibid., 1.5, in *Opuscula Theologica*, 9–12, cited in Rondet, *Gratia Christi*, 289.

redemption, grace does not confer upon us any supernatural gratuitous gift; it restores our broken free will, and enables us to do good works again.[53]

Because Baius compromised the necessity of grace before the Fall and the freedom of the will after it, Baianism was condemned quickly by Pope Pius IV in 1564.[54] But that condemnation was not the end of Catholic, post-Reformation Augustinianism. The torch was carried by Cornelius Otto Jansen (often referred to as Jansenius; 1585–1638), who followed Baius in general but corrected some of his excesses.[55] In Jansen's chief work, the posthumously published, *Augustinus*,[56] he admitted that there is a distinction between the natural use of our free will, and the supernatural use of our free will under the influence of grace; even for Adam and Eve, good works with an unaided free will would have given them no right or title to the beatific vision. Nevertheless, Jansen still found a way agree with Baius that the beatific vision was owed to our first parents: since they had a desire for it inscribed upon their nature, God was constrained to give them the grace to fulfill that desire.[57] Jansen thereby compromised the gratuity of grace on a metaphysical level, just as Baius had compromised it on a legal level.

Jansen also agreed with Baius that the fallen will is so wounded that any good work requires grace.[58] However, he differed from Baius on the purpose of grace, because he acknowledged that a human will, restored by grace but otherwise devoid of supernatural help, would not be enough to merit the beatific vision. Grace works by presenting us with an attraction towards a supernatural good that is so strong that our fallen will—which must choose whatever seems most desirable to it—cannot but choose

---

53. Rondet, *Gratia Christi*, 289.

54. Pope Pius IV, *Ex omnibus afflictionibus*, in *Enchiridion symbolorum*. English translation: *Compendium of Creeds, Definitions, and Declarations*; the full text of the condemnation can be found in Enchiridion symbolorum, definitionum et declarationum de rebus fidei et morum, 33rd edition, ed. Denzinger and Adolf Schönmetzer (1901–1980).

55. On the dependence of Jansen on Baius, see de Lubac, *Augustinianism and Modern Theology*, 36. On Jesuit opposition to Jansenism in general, see Pomplun, *Jesuit on the Roof*, 100–101.

56. Cornelius Jansen, *Augustinus*, 3 vols. (Louvain: Jacques Zegers, 1640).

57. Jansen, *De statu purae naturae* 1.2, in *Augustinus*, 2:685. See also Jansen. 1.15, in *Augustinus*, 2:745–52; De Lubac, *Augustinianism and Modern Theology*, 37–38. On Jansen's understanding of the effects of the Fall on the will, see Pomplun, *Jesuit on the Roof, 100*; Skirry, "Malebranche's Augustinianism," 32–33.

58. Jansen, *De gratia Christi Salvatoris* 4.1. in *Augustinus*, 3:15–18, 398.

grace.[59] He called this sort of grace "victorious delight" (*delectatio victrix*).[60] Victorious delight infallibly determines the will towards a specific action. However, it does so by conquering the will, not by cooperating with it.

Since Jansen denied the gratuity of grace where Baius had denied its necessity, and Jansen denied with Baius the freedom of the will after the Fall, Jansenism was condemned by successive popes throughout the seventeenth century.[61] Nevertheless, Jansenism survived these rebukes and took root in France because the way in which its view of concupiscence affected the way in which French Catholics tended to think of papal authority.[62] By and large, the French had always been reticent to acknowledge the temporal and spiritual authority of the pope in France.[63] Jansenism played to this reticence—it encouraged a distrust of centralized authority, because of the strength of concupiscence and the tendency towards fallibility to be found in fallen persons.

---

59. Ibid., 4.7, in *Augustinus*, 3:414. "Dico itaque juxta sancti Augustini mentem constantissimam et saepe declaratam, idcirco in ista cum tentationibus dimicatione, magnam adeoque majorem ac victricem delectationem caelestem esse necessariam, ut delectatio terrena superetur, quia alioquin voluntas tam magnas volendi vires adhibere non potest . . ." cf. de Lubac, *Augustinianism and Modern Theology*, 38–39; Skirry, "Malebranche's Augustinianism," 30–32. De Lubac succinctly summarizes: '[Jansen's] supralapsarian 'optimism' has determined his practical pessimism."

60. Jansen, *De gratia Christi Salvatoris* 4.6, in *Augustinus* 3:410–13, cited. in Rondet, *Gratia Christi*, 310.

61. Philips, *Church and Culture*, 103–4.

62. De Lubac, *Augustinianism and Modern Theology*, 33-35; Simmonds, "Jansenism," 25; Skirry, "Malebranche's Augustinianism," 28–29. Part of the reason that Jansenism had such a practical influence on French Catholics was that, unlike Baianism, Jansenism was concerned more with a reform of life from *within* the Roman Catholic Church than with opposing the Protestant Reformers outside of it. The Jansenists criticized the Jesuits, whose moral theology at the time was marked by casuistry, which could be used to find subtle ways of excusing people from sin, and probabilism, which permitted anyone to choose a course of action as long as some reasonable theologian could be found to support it. The focal point of the controversy was a volume published by Antoine Arnauld in 1643 attacking Jesuit confessors for indiscriminately encouraging penitents to receive daily communion without sufficient preparation. In response, Arnauld set out the need for a rigorous—though in practice, scrupulous—preparation for communion, on account of the depths of fallen man's woundedness. The book was Antoine Arnauld, *De la fréquente communion*; cf. Strayer, *Suffering Saints*; 58; Skirry, "Malebranche's Augustinianism," 27.

63. See Costigan, *The Consensus of the Church*, 6–7.

This French wariness of papal authority, known as Gallicanism,[64] developed in earnest as a theological movement in the late seventeenth century. At that time, French theologians attempted to codify their long-standing reservations towards the papacy,[65] so as to circumvent a particular papal condemnation of Jansenism: the bull, *Cum occasione* (1653), of Innocent X.[66] In that bull, the pope censured as heretical five propositions which were supposed to have been taken from Jansen's *Augustinus*. Jansen's followers argued that, while the five propositions in the bull were in fact heretical, the pope had no right and no power to declare that they accurately reflected anything that the Jansen actually said, or that Jansenists therefore actually believed.[67]

In order to oppose the condemnation, the French Clergy issued a *Declaration of the Clergy of France* on March 19, 1682, summarizing their principal reservations in four points: first, that God had given the pope spiritual authority but not temporal authority—*a fortiori* God did not give the pope authority over the temporal affairs of France; second, that there are limits to the spiritual power which the pope has over the Church in France—he cannot simply impose his will, his choices, or his teaching; third, that in addition to those limits, the pope has to observe the laws, customs and constitutions of France, along with the customary modes of interaction between the papacy and France; fourth, that the pope is not infallible, and that therefore his teaching is reformable; it only becomes infallible with the consent of the Church.[68] In the late eighteenth and early

---

64. McGrath, *Iustitia Dei*, 96. The attitude can be traced to the disputes between King Philip IV (1268–1314) and Pope Boniface VIII (c. 1230s–1303) over the temporal jurisdiction of the papacy. Philip's primary theological supporter was John of Paris, OP (John Quidort), whose *De regia potestate et papali* asserted the independence of temporal authority from ecclesiatical authority in temporal affairs. English translation: John of Paris, *On Royal and Papal Power*.

65. McCool, *Nineteenth-Century Scholasticism*, 21.

66. Phillips, *Church and Culture*, 122; Strayer, *Suffering Saints*, 69–71.

67. Ibid., 69–71. As Strayer notes, the argument was rendered moot by a subsequent bull of Pope Alexander VII, *Ad sacram*, which condemned the propositions not only as heretical in themselves, but also "as Jansen meant them."

68. Mention, ed., *Documents relatifs aux rapports du clergé avec la royauté*, 1:26–32. A distinction is often made in scholarship of this period between "political" Gallicanism, which emphasizes the independence of temporal authority from spiritual authority, and "spiritual," "ecclesiastical," or "religious" Gallicanism, which emphasizes the independence of local spiritual authority from universal spiritual authority.

nineteenth centuries, the four Gallicanist principles were widely received among the French clergy as normative.[69]

In 1691, Pope Alexander VIII nullified the *Declaration of the Clergy of France*.[70] In doing so, he did not remove the question of the nature of Church unity from discussion among Catholic theologians any more than the Council of Trent removed the question of the nature of the relationship between the free will and grace from discussion; he merely nullified the declaration *qua* declaration, and so dissolved any binding character it may have seemed to exert upon the French people.[71] There remained yet for the Catholic Church formally to decide whether to follow the Jesuits, the Augustinians, or some other way. Even when Jansenism received its definitive papal condemnation in 1794, that condemnation focused more on grace and free will than it did on the nature of the Church; only the most extreme Gallican propositions about the Church were censured.[72] Much like the conclusion of the *De auxiliis* controversy left the Catholic Church with two rival opinions about grace and free will, with no determination between them, the conclusion of the Jansenist controversy left the Catholic Church with two rival opinions about the unity of the Church.

Ultramontanism and Church Unity:
Pastor Aeternus (July 18, 1870)

Thus, in the nineteenth century, the Roman Catholic Church inherited two very different Augustinianisms. On the one hand, the Jesuits proposed a free will that was absolute, grace which was extrinsic to the soul, and a unified Church which formed a society modeled on human states, which was led by the pope as the sole absolute monarch on earth. Following the *Declaration of the Clergy of France*, this Jesuit-inspired attitude assumed the title of "Ultramontanism," ("beyond the mountains") referring to the transalpine allegiance of its adherents to the person of the pope.[73] On the surface, it seemed to preserve the three Augustinian themes, but under the

---

69. Edgar Hocedez, *Histoire de la théologie au xixe siècle*, 2:149–51, cited. in McCool, *Nineteenth-Century Scholasticism*, 22.

70. Costigan, *The Consensus of the Church*, 19–20. For the text of the annulment, see DH 2285.

71. Ibid., 20–21.

72. For the text of the condemnation, see Pius VI, Auctorem fidei (DH 2600–2700).

73. See Costigan, *The Consensus of the Church*, 5–6.

surface, it was not immune from criticism: first, from the Dominicans, who wondered whether it sufficiently protected the necessity of grace; second, from the Augustinians, who wondered whether it sufficiently accounted for human sinfulness; third, in terms of the manner in which it considered the pope as an absolute monarch: does this not in some way impinge upon the freedom of Christians which the Jesuits strove so hard to protect? On the other hand, the Augustinians proposed a free will that was vitiated by sin, a grace which conquered the soul, and a Church in which authority followed the divisions of the State. It had the benefit of protecting the sovereignty of God and acknowledging the seriousness of sin, but at the cost of upholding the freedom of the will and the unity of the Church—two of the essential Augustinian themes bequeathed to the Catholic Church in the post-Reformation period.

When the First Vatican Council met from 1869–1870, the Council Fathers intended to take up the question of the Church in the manner similar to that in which the Council Fathers of Trent had taken up the question of free will and grace. They determined to declare, for the first time in an ecumenical council, the nature of the Church as such. After a first draft was discussed, *Supremi Pastoris*, it was decided that there would be two documents: the first would discuss the pope; the second the Church as a whole.[74] Only the first, *Pastor Aeternus*, materialized. To this day it bears the subtitle, "*First* Dogmatic Constitution on the Church of Christ." (emphasis added), even though there is no "*Second* Dogmatic Constitution on the Church of Christ." It was promulgated in a rush at the outbreak of the Franco-Prussian War; the constitution on the rest of the Church had to be abandoned.

At the time of the promulgation of *Pastor Aeternus*, the influence of Gallicanism had languished.[75] The result was that *Pastor Aeternus* was deliberately crafted to oppose the *Declaration of the Clergy of France*, declaring in its four chapters that 1) Peter alone was the Prince of the Apostles and received directly from Christ jurisdiction over the Church; 2) the Pope succeeds Peter to this primacy; 3) the Pope possesses the fullness of the power of jurisdiction over faith and morals, as well as discipline and government in the Church; and 4) that "when in discharge of the office of Pastor and Teacher of all Christians, by virtue of his supreme Apostolic

---

74. The decision to issue two declarations was made on April 27, 1870. See Granfield, "The Church as *Societas Perfecta*," *Church History* 48 (1979) 441.

75. Costigan, *The Consensus of the Church*, 5.

authority, he defines a doctrine regarding faith or morals to be held by the Universal Church, by the divine assistance promised to him in blessed Peter ... " he possesses an infallibility guaranteed by Christ. The Council Fathers were particularly keen to oppose this last chapter to the fourth assertion of the *Declaration of the Clergy of France*. Where the *Declaration* said that the teaching of the pope only became irreformable with the consent of the Church; *Pastor Aeternus* defined that papal teaching given under the conditions set forth was "irreformable of itself, and not by the consent of the Church."[76]

In one sense, *Pastor Aeternus* seemed to canonize the ultramontanist understanding of the pope. However, while *Pastor Aeternus* did certainly canonize many of the elements of an ultramontanist understanding of the papacy, it did not canonize the ultramontanist system as a whole, nor therefore did it canonize the centrality of the papacy *as understood* by that system. It might have done so, if the Franco-Prussian War had not broken out; both drafts for the Second Constitution on the Church described the Church in terms akin to Suárez, and so made clear the place of the pope within the Church as an absolute monarch along the lines of temporal monarchs.[77] But the untimely interruption of the Council Fathers proved, perhaps by God's Providence, to have been unexpectedly timely; there was yet an opportunity for the development of an alternative way of recognizing the centrality of the papacy in the Church, one which accorded more consistently with the freedom will.

Augustinianism and Church Unity:
Lumen Gentium **(November 21, 1964)**

In the wake of Vatican I, a renewal of Jesuit and Dominican Thomism took place, spurred on by the Council's declarations which were favorable to post-Reformation Thomism. That renewal began in earnest with the promulgation of Pope Leo XIII's Encyclical letter, *Aeterni Patris* (August 4, 1879). Leo XIII had received his theological formation from Jesuit Thomists,[78] and he taught in *Aeterni Patris* that Thomism could serve as a salutary remedy for a world struggling with rationalism, empiricism, and fideism. Throughout the late-nineteenth and early-twentieth centuries, this form of

76. Ibid., 2.
77. Granfield, "The Church as *Societas Perfecta*," 431.
78. Cf. McCool, *Nineteenth-Century Scholasticism*, 226–28.

Thomism, now referred to as *neo-scholasticism*, predominated in Catholic seminaries and universities.

Yet however much neo-scholasticism, inspired by post-Reformation Thomism, may have been the dominant force in Roman Catholic theology in the early twentieth century, that period also witnessed the beginning of a retrieval of other sources from the theological tradition. This movement, known as *ressourcement*, criticized neo-scholastic Thomism for relying too heavily on the theologians of the post-Reformation era, instead of the sources in the theological tradition which those theologians used themselves, like Augustine and Aquinas. Some *ressourcement* theologians, like Jean Daniélou, SJ (1905–1974),[79] and Yves Congar, OP (1904–995),[80] thought that the post-Reformation period in Catholic theology had little to offer and proposed abandoning that period in favor of previous ones.[81] Others, like Henri de Lubac, SJ (1896–1991), thought that all periods in the theological tradition had something to offer, it was only that sometimes the best resources from a given period were those which had been overlooked.[82]

Looking back on the history of the controversies on grace and the Church, de Lubac found one such forgotten resource in the theological tradition of the Order of the Hermits of Saint Augustine (known in English as the "Augustinian Hermits" or "Austin Friars").[83] Their theological tradition, often described as "Aegidian" because of its founder, Giles of Rome, OESA ("Aegidius Romanus" in Latin; d. 1316), saw a kernel of truth in Jansenism:

79. On Daniélou's place in the *ressourcement* movement, see Bernard Pottier, "Daniélou and the Twentieth-Century Patristic Renewal," in *Ressourcement: A Movement for Renewal in Twentieth-Century Catholic Theology*, ed. Gabriel Flynn and Paul Murray (New York: Oxford, 2012), 250–62.

80. On Congar's place in the *ressourcement* movement, see Gabriel Flynn, "*Ressourcement*, Ecumenism, and Pneumatology: The Contribution Yves Congar to *Nouvelle Theology*," in *Ressourcement*, 219–35.

81. Daniélou, 'Les orientations présentes de la pensée religieuse,' Études 79 (1946) 7; Yves Congar, *Journal d'un théologien: 1946–1956* (Paris: Cerf, 2001), 59, cited in Francesca Murphy, *Art and Intellect in the Philosophy of Étienne Gilson* (Columbia: University of Missouri Press, 2004), 227. Congar in particular was inspired by a movement of Patristic renewal in nineteenth- century German Roman Catholic Theology centered on Johann Adam Möhler (1796–1838) and the Tübingen School.

82. On the place of de Lubac in the *ressourcement* movement, see Jacob Wood, "Ressourcement," in *The T&T Clark Companion to Henri de Lubac*, ed. Jordan Hillebert (Edinburgh: T. & T. Clark, 2016) (forthcoming).

83. De Lubac, *Surnaturel: Études historiques* (Paris: Aubier, 1946), 164–165. De Lubac calls this tradition the "Augustinian School *par excellence*."

the desire for grace is constitutive of nature, and our understanding of free will, grace, and the Church, should be built upon this desire. However, unlike the Jansenists, the members of the Aegidian tradition also maintained that an Augustinianism of desire could be articulated without compromising the freedom of the will or the unity of the Church.

In the period after Jansenism, the principal representative of the Aegidian tradition was Giovanni Lorenzo Berti, OESA (1696-1766).[84] Berti gave the classic exposition of Aegidian thought in his 10-volume work, *On the Theological Disciplines*.[85] He agreed with Jansen that man's natural desire for the vision of God is constitutive of human nature;[86] but he also criticized Jansen's conclusion that the grace which brings us to that vision is therefore owed to human nature: since the vision of God is outside of our natural powers, God is absolutely free to withhold it.[87] Berti proposed a mediate position: God *could*, absolutely speaking, withhold grace, but we can hardly imagine that a Provident God *would*, since he knows that grace is the only means to our final end.[88] We can, Berti thinks, have confidence that the mercy of God will fulfill our heart's greatest desires without compromising the gratuity of that mercy.

Berti also agreed with Jansen that grace can be thought of as *delectatio victrix*.[89] But where Jansen framed the efficacity of grace as a conquest of force, Berti framed it as a conquest of love. Instead of agreeing with Jansen that the fallen will is completely vitiated by sin and needs to be ruled by grace, Berti sought a middle way between Suárez's optimism and Jansen's pessimism. The fallen will is still free, and still capable of some limited, temporal good;[90] without grace it can even perform acts of natural virtue,

---

84. Unfortunately, no introduction to Berti's life and works has yet been written.

85. Berti, *De theologicis disciplinis*, 10 vols. (Naples: Migliaccio, 1776-84).

86. Berti, *De theologicis disciplinis*, 3.1.1-2 [Naples 1:66-68]. Berti supports this argument on the basis of his understanding of what it means for man to be in the *imago dei*. The *imago dei* is something natural in man. On account of this image man is naturally capable of seeing God, and desires to do so. See Berti, *De theologicis disciplinis*, 12.7.2 [Naples 3:31B]; *Additamentum ad lib.* 12, cap. 2 [Naples 3:78A].

87. His response to this principle begins at ibid., *Additamentum*, cap. 2 [Naples 3:79B]. Berti's position was much controverted in his day. It was thought by many to be close to Jansenism, although it was never formally condemned as such. See Hardon, History and Theology of Grace, 87.

88. Berti, *De theologicis disciplinis*, 13.3 [Naples: 3:101B-102A].

89. See Berti, *De theologicis disciplinis*, 14.8.2 [Naples 3:178B-180B].

90. Berti, *De theologicis disciplinis*, 18.2.1 [Naples 4:4B].

which, while they do not merit the vision of God, are still good in themselves.[91] "Practically speaking," that tends not to happen because the pull of concupiscence is so strong, but still it is technically possible.[92] Prevenient grace frees the will more completely by a premotion, which is given prior to our deliberation,[93] and which excites the will towards charity.[94] That first motion does not force the will to choose grace; technically, we could still convince ourselves to refuse it. But again, practically speaking, God's love is so delightful that it infallibly achieves its purpose in us.[95]

De Lubac made use of the Aegidian tradition to propose a new vision of the Church in the twentieth century, a vision was taken up by the Catholic Church in *Lumen Gentium*, its Constitution on the Church at the Second Vatican Council (1962–65), and used to complete the work begun at Vatican I. For de Lubac, the Church is not Suárez's ecclesial nation-state, brought together by the sole monarch of divine right, nor yet is the Church a Jansenist collection of states brought within the Church and yet so vitiated by sin that they remain yet alien from one another. It is, rather, a *communion* of people, whose desires have been healed by grace, and who therefore freely and willing enter into communion with the one God in one ecclesial community.[96]

Lumen Gentium elaborated on that ecclesiology of communion. It grounded the unity of the Church not in the pope *qua* Vicar of Christ but in the unity of the three persons of the Trinity,[97] into a participation of which the Church is drawn as the Body of Christ by the Holy Spirit.[98] The pope has his place in the unity of this body; *Lumen Gentium* reaffirms that he is

---

91. Berti, *De theologicis disciplinis*, 18.3 [Naples 4:16B–17A].

92. Ibid.

93. In 14.8.4 [Naples 3:182B], Berti goes on to locate the difference between his *delectatio victrix* and Jansen's precisely in the fact that Jansen's does not free the will to assent so much as it is forces the will to assent.

94. Berti, *De theologicis disciplinis*, 14.8.2 [Naples 3:180A]. "Etenim si gratia accipiatur ex parte Dei, quatenus est ipsa Misericordia movens, et caritatem inspirans, nullatenus cum nostra deliberation coniuncta est . . . Si consideretur ex parte nostra, est ipsa dilectio simul a Dei inspiratione et voluntate nostra promanans; a voluntate tamen, ut a Deo intime praesente praemota . . ."

95. Berti, *De theologicis disciplinis*, [Naples 3:182B].

96. De Lubac introduced this point in *Catholicism: Christ and the Common Destiny of Man*. He developed it in Henri de Lubac, *The Splendor of the Church*.

97. *Lumen Gentium*, 5.

98. Ibid., 7.

the focal point of Christian unity.[99] But he does not exercise that office as an imposition on Christian freedom, an absolute sovereign imposed upon unwilling subjects; he is, rather, the focal point of a bond of "unity, charity, and peace,"[100] which is a gift bestowed upon the entire Church and willingly received by it, not an office imposed on it.

Conclusion

The Reformation began a conversation. It challenged the Roman Catholic Church to articulate an Augustinianism, which could account in an integral way for the freedom of the will, the necessity of grace, and the unity of the Church. That was a difficult challenge. Ultimately it took four and a half centuries for the Roman Catholic Church to give its first complete answer at Vatican II.

Many things changed within the Catholic Church in the years between the Reformation and Vatican II. Not the least of these was the Catholic Church's attitude towards the communities of the Reformation. In a way, that attitude was dictated by the Catholic Church's understanding of itself. When many Catholics saw the Church as possessed of the sole absolute monarch on earth, dialogue with the communities of the Reformation seemed a distraction; does a king of divine right dialogue with disobedient subjects? But the ecclesiology of Vatican II gave the Catholic Church an understanding of itself which was at once more consistent, more profound, and more humble: seeing the Petrine Office and the unity attendant upon it as a gift from God to be shared in and reconciled with freedom and grace, not an office to be imposed.

In the years since Vatican II, this renewal of self-understanding has enabled ecumenical progress to proceed at a pace which would have been unthinkable a century ago. One of the most significant fruits of this progress has been the *Joint Declaration on the Doctrine of Justification* made between the Lutheran World Federation and the Pontifical Council for Promoting Christian Unity, in which Catholics recognized the importance of the will in the Lutheran doctrine of justification, and Lutherans recognized the primacy of grace in the Catholic doctrine of justification. That declaration made a bold move towards healing the ecclesial divisions brought about during the Reformation, by returning to one of the principal disagreements

99. Ibid., 23.
100. Ibid., 22.

that began it in search of reconciliation. Although the *Joint Declaration* did not resolve every disagreement between Catholics and Lutherans on the doctrine of justification,[101] and so full reconciliation remains a goal to be pursued, we can say that it courageously forged the path along which full reconciliation will one day be achieved. For, while the relationship between grace and the will is famously difficult to articulate, the history of the Catholic Church since the Reformation shows that it is this difficult mystery upon which the unity of the Church stands or falls, both in dogma and in dialogue.

Bibliography

Arnauld, Antoine. *De la fréquente* communion. Paris: Antoine Vitré, 1643.
Aquinas, Thomas. *Opera Omnia*. Vol. 7. Rome, 1892.
Aristotle. "Politics." In *The Basic Works of Aristotle*, ed. Richard McKeon. New York: Modern Library, 2013.
Baius, Michael. *De meritis operum* 1.4. In *Opuscula Theologica*. Louvain: Bogard, 1566.
Báñez, Domingo. "De vera et legitima Concordia liberi arbitrii create cum auxiliis gratiae Dei efficaciter moventis humanam voluntatem," 2.1.4. In *Comentarios inéditos a la Prima Secundae de Santo Tomás*. 3 vols. Biblioteca de teólogos españoles 9, 11, 14. Salamanca: n.p., 1948.
Báñez, Domingo. *Scholastica Commentaria in Primam Partem Summa Theologicae S. Thomae Aquinatis*. Madrid: FGDA, 1934.
Bellarmine, Robert." De controversiis christianae fidei adversus hujus temporis haereticos," 3.2. In *Opera Omnia*, 2:75. Naples: Giuseppe Giuliano, 1856–62.
Clayton, Lawrence. *Bartolomé de las Casas: A Biography*. New York: Cambridge, 2012.
Costigan, Richard. *The Consensus of the Church and Papal Infallibility: A Study in the Background of Vatican I*. Washington, DC: Catholic University of America Press, 2005.
Cuadrado, José Ángel García. *Domingo Báñez (1528–1604): Introducción a su obra filosófica y teológica*. Pamplona: Servicio de Publicaciones de la Universidad de Navarra, 1999.
Denzinger, Heinrich and Peter Hünermann, eds., *Enchiridion symbolorum, definitionum et declarationum de rebus fidei et morum*. 43rd ed. Freiburg im Breisgau: Herder, 2010. English translation: *Compendium of Creeds, Definitions, and Declarations on Matters of Faith and Morals*, eds. Robert Fastiggi and Anne Englund Nash. San Francisco: Ignatius, 2012.
Donnelly, Philip. "Baius and Baianism." In *The New Catholic Encyclopedia*. 2nd ed. Detroit: Gale, 2003, 2:19.
Granfield, Patrick. "The Church as *Societas Perfecta* in the Schemata of Vatican I." *Church History* 48 (1979) 441.

---

101. See "Response of the Catholic Church to the Joint Declaration of the Catholic Church and the Lutheran World Federation on the Doctrine of Justification." http://www.vatican.va/roman_curia/pontifical_councils/chrstuni/documents/rc_pc _chrstuni_doc_01081998_off-answer-catholic_en.html.

Hardon, John. *History and Theology of Grace: The Catholic Teaching on Divine Grace.* Ave Maria, FL: Sapientia, 2002.
James I. "*A Premonition to All most Mightie Monarchies, Kings, Free Princes, and States of Christendome.*" In *The Political Works of James I*, edited by Charles McIlwain, 110–68. Cambridge: Harvard University Press, 1918.
Jansen, Cornelius. *Augustinus*, 3 vols. Louvain: Zegers, 1640.
John of Paris, *On Royal and Papal Power.* Translated by J. A. Watt. Toronto: PIMS, 2002.
Lubac, Henri de. *Augustinianism and Modern Theology.* Translated by Lancelot Sheppard. New York: Crossroads, 2000.
———. *Catholicism: Christ and the Common Destiny of Man.* Translated by Lancelot Sheppard and Elizabeth Englund. San Francisco: Ignatius, 1988.
———. *The Splendor of the Church.* Translated by Michael Mason. San Francisco: Ignatius, 1999.
———. *Surnaturel: Études historiques.* Paris: Aubier, 1946.
Luther, Martin. *De servo arbitrio ad Erasmum Roterodamum.* Wittenburg: Johannes Lufft, 1525; ET = *On the Bondage of the Will.* Translated by J. I. Packer and O. L. Johnston. Westwood, NJ: Revell, 1957.
MacGregor, Kirk R. *Luis de Molina: The Life and Theology of the Founder of Middle Knowledge.* Grand Rapids: Zondervan, 2015.
Malloy, Christopher. *Engrafted into Christ: A Critique of the Joint Declaration.* American University Studies. Series VII, Theology and Religion 233. New York: Lang, 2005.
McCool, Gerald. *Nineteenth-Century Scholasticism: The Search for a Unitary Method.* New York: Fordham University Press, 1989.
McGrath, Alistair. *Iustitia Dei.* New York: Cambridge, 1998.
Mention, Léon, ed. *Documents relatifs aux rapports du clergé avec la royauté de 1682 à 1705*, 1:26–32. 3 vols. Paris: Picard, 1893,
Molina, Luis de. *Concordia liberi arbitrii cum gratiae donis, divina praescientia, providentia, praedestinatione, et reprobatione, ad nonnullos primae partis D. Thomae articulos.* Lisbon: Ribeiro, 1588.
Murphy, Francesca. *Art and Intellect in the Philosophy of Étienne Gilson.* Columbia: University of Missouri Press, 2004.
Philips, Henry. *Church and Culture in Seventeenth-Century France.* New York: Cambridge University Press, 1997.
Pomplun, Trent. *Jesuit on the Roof of the World: Ippolito Desideri's Mission to Tibet.* New York: Oxford University Press, 2010.
Rondet, Henri. *Gratia Christi: Essai d'histoire du dogma et de théologie dogmatique.* Paris: Beauchesne, 1948.
Saak, Erik. *Creating Augustine: Interpreting Augustine and Augustinianism in the Later Middle Ages.* New York: Oxford University Press, 2012.
Salas, Victor, and Robert Fastiggi. "Introduction: Francisco Suárez, the Man and His Work." In *A Companion to Francisco Suárez.* Brill's Companions to the Christian Tradition 53. Leiden: Brill, 2014.
Simmonds, Gemma. "Jansenism: an Early *Ressourcement* Movement?" In *Ressourcement: A Movement for Renewal in Twentieth-Century Catholic Theology*, edited by Gabriel Flynn and Paul D. Murray, 25. New York: Oxford, 2012.
Skirry, Jason. "Malebranche's Augustinianism and the Mind's Perfection." PhD. diss., University of Pennsylvania, 2010.

Strayer, Brian. *Suffering Saints: Jansenists and Convulsionnaires in France, 1640–1799.* Portland, OR: Sussex Academic, 2008.

Suárez, Francisco. "Defensio Fidei Catholicae adverus Anglicanae Sectae Errores." 99 Eugene, OR: Sussex Academic, 2008.

———. *Opera Omnia.* Vol. 24. Paris: Vivès, 1859.

Tanner, Norman. *Council of Trent, Decretum de iustificatione.* In *Decrees of the Ecumenical Councils,* 2:672. 2 vol. Washington, DC: Georgetown University Press, 1990.

Warfield, B. B. *Calvin and Augustine.* Philadelphia: Presbyterian & Reformed, 1956.

www.ingramcontent.com/pod-product-compliance
Lightning Source LLC
Chambersburg PA
CBHW020855160426
43192CB00007B/938